A Book of Faith Seeking Understanding

A Book of Faith Seeking Understanding

Fifty-Two Lord's Day Readings

PHILIP JOHN FISK

Foreword by Kenneth P. Minkema

WIPF & STOCK · Eugene, Oregon

A BOOK OF FAITH SEEKING UNDERSTANDING
Fifty-Two Lord's Day Readings

Copyright © 2021 Philip John Fisk. All rights reserved. Except for brief quotations in critical publications or reviews, no part of this book may be reproduced in any manner without prior written permission from the publisher. Write: Permissions, Wipf and Stock Publishers, 199 W. 8th Ave., Suite 3, Eugene, OR 97401.

Wipf & Stock
An Imprint of Wipf and Stock Publishers
199 W. 8th Ave., Suite 3
Eugene, OR 97401

www.wipfandstock.com

PAPERBACK ISBN: 978-1-6667-3167-5
HARDCOVER ISBN: 978-1-6667-2438-7
EBOOK ISBN: 978-1-6667-2439-4

11/10/21

Unless otherwise indicated, Scripture quotations are from the New Revised Standard Version Bible. Copyright© 1989 by the National Council of the Churches of Christ in the United States of America. Used by permission. All rights reserved worldwide.

Scripture quotations marked (KJV) are taken from The Authorized (King James) Version. Rights in the Authorized Version in the United Kingdom are vested in the Crown. Reproduced by permission of the Crown's patentee, Cambridge University Press.

Scripture quotations marked (ESV) are from The ESV® Bible (The Holy Bible, English Standard Version®), copyright © 2001 by Crossway, a publishing ministry of Good News Publishers. Used by permission. All rights reserved."

*For Cynthia Joy,
Ashley and David, Zachary and Aubrey, Jonathan and Fabia,
and grandchildren*

Contents

Foreword by Kenneth P. Minkema		ix
Preface		xi
Front Matter Endnotes		xiv
1	Archetypal Theology	1
2	Ectypal Theology	3
3	The Logos, Life, and Light	5
4	God's Knowledge of Approbation	7
5	God's Knowledge of Simple Understanding	9
6	God's Knowledge of Vision	11
7	God's Negative Indifference	13
8	God's Double Glory	15
9	God's Double Plotline	17
10	God's Double Gift	19
11	God's Physical Influx	21
12	God's Passions and Immutability 1	23
13	God's Passions and Immutability 2	25
14	Christ Our Surety	27
15	God's Foreknowledge and Human Freedom	29
16	The Will: Producible versus Produced	31
17	The Priority of Nature versus Time	33
18	The Noble Cause	35
19	The Soul's Power of the Will	37
20	Shipwrecked and God's Physical Predetermination 1	39
21	Shipwrecked and God's Physical Predetermination 2	41
22	Prayer for Such a Time as This	43
23	Christian Fate	45

Contents

24	Sifting Providence Down to the Pure Bran 1	47
25	Sifting Providence Down to the Pure Bran 2	49
26	Sifting Providence Down to the Pure Bran 3	51
27	*Summè Perfectus et Summum Bonum*	53
28	*Nunc Aeternitatis*	55
29	The Neutral Proposition	57
30	*Instantia Rationis*	59
31	The Residue of the Spirit	61
32	A Double Conversion	63
33	Can the Justified Be Condemned?	65
34	The Virgin Mystery	67
35	Can the Past Be Contingent?	69
36	The Euthyphro Mystery	71
37	God's Double Will 1	73
38	God's Double Will 2	75
39	The Mystery of God's Permissive Will	77
40	The Mystery of the Messiah's Impeccability	79
41	The Mystery of Evil	81
42	God's Best of All Possible Worlds	83
43	The Mystery of God's Supposed Middle Knowledge	85
44	The Mystery of *Creabilis, Creandus,* and *Creatus*	87
45	The Law of Truth	89
46	The Law of Justice	91
47	The Law of Wisdom	93
48	The Square of Opposition	95
49	The Square of Opposition Revisited	97
50	The Essence of Free Choice	99
51	The Self-Determining Power of the Will	101
52	God Is No Minister of Fate	103
Chapter Endnotes		105
Bibliography		121
Name Index		129
Scripture Index		133

Foreword

WHILE THERE ARE MANY positive directions that the churches of the Reformation, now evolved into modern Protestantism in all its variety, have taken, there are several unfortunate side effects. One such side effect is the decline of creedal and confessional churches, and, along with that, a lack of appreciation for historic creeds and confessions. I was brought up in the Christian Reformed Church, solidly grounded in the Canons of Dordt, the Belgic Confession, and the Heidelberg Catechism. Of course, when one is young, one often doesn't appreciate the history, wisdom, and even beauty—yes, beauty—of such documents. I was no exception. Only later in life did I realize what I had had, and how much I missed having worship and catechesis based on those classic expressions of faith.

The Heidelberg Catechism of 1563 was formatted in a question-and-answer manner. Rather than relying on rote memorization to instill religious teaching, the writers of the Catechism, drawing on new theories of human formation and knowing, saw that learning was a two-way process, a dialogue between teacher and student. For each Sabbath, or "Lord's Day," there was a question and answer to be considered, taking the individual believer and the congregation through the fundamentals of the faith each church year. The volume you hold in your hands is similarly laid out, Heidelberg Catechism style, into fifty-two "Lord's Days." It also addresses basic, difficult questions of divine and human action and interaction, though centered around a common theme. That theme is one of especial weight in today's world: the origin and nature of evil.

Foreword

We live in a time when it is easy—too easy—to label, and thereby cancel, any other person, idea, or cause as evil. Religious truth—political truth, for that matter—is at the mercy of personal, subjective, visceral, even vicarious experience, verging on the solipsistic, cast adrift from historical and social moorings. Perhaps we've made an idol of self-determination at the expense of seeing ourselves as part of the flow of history and as members of a commonweal or a series of commonweals. Seeking something to blame for catastrophes—pandemics, racism, mass shootings, insurrections—we deflect culpability from ourselves and try to blame God, fate, what have you.

The meditations presented here are a series of dialogues, conversations with religious figures of the past—some well known, some not so much, but worth knowing. To imagine how you would have a conversation with someone in the past can be a handy way to humanize them. I have long worked on the eighteenth-century British American theologian Jonathan Edwards, and I often wonder, if he were to appear now, how I would explain things to him, such as the internal combustion engine, or radio, or air travel. Fortunately, the author here has taken a more serious approach. In created dialogues with stalwarts of the Protestant past, he connects the reader to a rich and thoughtful body of thought and to an expanse of issues—and solutions—regarding divinity and humanity, intellect and faith. Each dialogue ends with a "commission," a lesson and biblical texts on which to meditate.

I commend to you this guide containing wise and pious voices of the past debating central issues of human existence. May it be a means for you to be led in the path from sin to salvation and service.

KENNETH P. MINKEMA
Jonathan Edwards Center
Yale University

Preface

*Amicus Plato, amicus Aristoteles, sed magis
amica veritas.*
Let Plato be a friend, let Aristotle be a friend, but
even more let truth be a friend.[1]

THE CHURCH IS IN crisis today. Superficial answers are the majority report when it comes to conversations about what the church has taught about whether God is the author of evil. There are, of course, excellent books written about the problem of evil and other philosophical and theological challenges that have faced the church. Very often, though, if authors turn at all to the early modernity of the seventeenth century for answers to questions, it is the well-known philosophers and mathematicians who are quoted, such as Thomas Hobbes (1588–1679), René Descartes (1596–1650), Blaise Pascal (1623–62), John Locke (1632–1704), and Gottfried Wilhelm Leibniz (1646–1716), none of whom had appointments at a university. This book draws exclusively from my own research into the primary sources of the neglected, if not forgotten, seventeenth and early eighteenth-century university professors, rectors, presidents, and bishops—to name a few, William Ames, Gisbertus Voetius, Adriaan Heereboord, Peter van Mastricht, Charles Morton, and Samuel Willard. To be sure, there are exceptions, such as the prominent New England theologian Jonathan Edwards (1703–58), who did have a short-lived appointment at the College of New Jersey, marking the end of his life. Relatedly, each university professor, rector, or theologian with whom I engage in the Lord's Day readings was either a rector at Harvard or Yale College, or part of Edwards's reading and Reformed theological heritage, with few exceptions.

My quest is to display their teaching on how they attempted to exonerate God from the charge that he is the author of evil. What makes this book of faith seeking understanding different are the sophisticated scholastic distinctions that I introduce, distinctions which often are discarded and discounted as unnecessarily masking an otherwise vibrant Christian faith with dry logic and rigidly forensic doctrines. But the resurgence of interest in Protestant scholasticism in the last decades has, arguably, proven otherwise.

To this end, I have chosen to cast the fifty-two Lord's Day readings into narrative form, like that of Plato's dialogues. I trust that the narrative will engage a greater number of readers than otherwise may be the case, without sacrificing content to form. The dialectic style also affords the opportunity to tease out the meaning and significance of scholastic distinctions, distinctions that are crucial to understanding how the classic Protestant tradition of the Christian faith defended God against the charge that he is the author of evil. The theological and philosophical distinctions that the church has taught in the past deserve to be heard and pondered by the church today. These fifty-two Lord's Day readings intend to fill the gap.

The culture of dialectic and debate had its origins in the medieval culture of disputation. Anselm (ca. 1033–1109) practiced the art of dialectic not only as disputation, but also as private meditation, an inner dialogue. Indeed, it was Anselm who successfully "pioneered" and demonstrated the power of both reason and dialectic in Christian faith seeking understanding.[2]

The composition of the dialogue between Anselm and his interlocutor, Boso, in *Why God Became Man* (*Cur Deus Homo*, 1098) famously exemplifies the demonstrative purpose and method of this rational art. Novikoff points out that this is but one of the seven literary works by Anselm that takes the form of dialogue.[3] The culture of scholastic method and practice in the universities, among the Dominicans—who institutionalized the art of debate and disputation in the education of their preachers—in medieval Jewish-Christian debates, and among poets introduced new forums for debate beyond the schools, in private audiences, and in the public square.

Wherever possible, I give a reference to the primary sources. If there is a primary source with a modern critical edition of the text, usually with the original Latin text alongside the English or French, with commentary, then I give the reference. When I discuss a Harvard or Yale commencement broadside sheet, which lists the Latin theses and names of respondents, I provide a translation and give an online address where readers can consult the broadside sheets for themselves.

I now invite you to eavesdrop on these literary renditions of dialogues that I narrate in the spirit of the motto of the faculty of theology where I teach: "faith seeking understanding" (*fides quaerens intellectum*), which is taken from the original title of Anselm's *Proslogium*.[4] The Lord's Day readings are written in this same spirit of prayer and reverence when approaching God and attempting to understand who he is. In the tradition of Anselm, John Duns Scotus (1266–1308) prayed:

> May the First Principle of things grant me to believe, to understand and to reveal what may please his majesty and may raise our minds to contemplate him.
>
> O Lord our God, true teacher that you are, when Moses your servant asked you for your name that he might proclaim it to the children of Israel, you, knowing what the mind of mortals could grasp of you, replied: "I am who am," thus disclosing your blessed name. You are truly what it means to be, you are the whole of what it means to exist. This, if it be possible for me, I should like to know by way of demonstration. Help me then, O Lord, as I investigate how much our natural reason can learn about that true being which you are if we begin with the being which you have predicated of yourself.[5]

Front Matter Endnotes

1. Ames, *Technometry*, 107 (§77). The likely origin of the later adaptation of the motto is from Aristotle, *Nicomachean Ethics*, in McKeon, *Basic Works*, 939 (1096a15). For more on this motto, see Morison, *Founding of Harvard College*, 330–31.
2. Novikoff, *Medieval Culture of Disputation*, 225–27.
3. Novikoff, *Medieval Culture of Disputation*, 42.
4. Anselme, *Monologion, Proslogion*, 230.
5. Duns Scotus, *Treatise on God*, 2.

1
Archetypal Theology

"TODAY, I AM GOING to teach you about a mystery of our faith," said University of Franeker professor William Ames (1576–1633). "Mysteries that no one can unfold."

"It sounds as if there are limits to faith seeking understanding," I said.

"Indeed, there are," he said. "In Latin, the word *typus* means a stamp, an impression, a character, or a mark—typed on a piece of paper, for instance."

"What, then, is the mystery?" I asked.

"The mystery enters in when you add the word *archē*, which refers us back to the beginning, the first principle, the original pattern of all patterns, as it were. Archetypal theology speaks of the infinite first kind of knowledge that belongs to God alone," Ames said. "Leiden University professor Franciscus Junius (1545–1602) wrote in *A Treatise on True Theology* that archetypal theology is 'the divine wisdom of divine matters. Indeed, we stand in awe before this and do not seek to trace it out.'[1] In fact, in *A Scholastical and Methodical Institution of the Common Places of Divinity*, Leiden professor Lucas Trelcatius Jr. (1573–1607) said that since archetypal knowledge belongs to God alone and is the 'first pattern, which in God is of God himself,' and is that which he knows in himself, he refrained from calling it *divinity*. For divinity is that which we can study and know; it is the 'stamp' of the first pattern, called ectypal

1

theology. 'But God and that which is in God is the selfsame in a simple essence.' Trelcatius went on to explain that God knows himself by one 'indivisible and unchangeable act.'[2] There is no passing of time in God's knowledge of himself. As I wrote in *The Marrow of Theology*, 'God knows all things by genesis, not analysis.'[3] Trelcatius also wrote, as I did, that God knows 'all and singular things by himself.'"[4]

"I suppose there would never be enough time to finish, if God were to begin to tell us about himself," I said, "let alone about his knowledge of all things that could come to pass in time."

Commission: Ponder anew our God, who is the pattern of all patterns, the genesis of all beginnings, the archetype of truth, goodness, and beauty to be revealed in Christ and in us.

Deut 29:29; Ps 147:5; Rom 11:33

2

Ectypal Theology

LAST LORD'S DAY, WE had an exercise in understanding the *archē* of archetype. But I asked Professor Ames to tell me how the *type* of archetype fits in with God's knowledge of created things.

"Trelcatius wrote," said Ames, "that 'the stamp' (*ectypus*)—or, as I would add, 'a certain refraction'[5] of God's knowledge—is made known to us in our very nature as people created by God. Trelcatius said that God blesses us with the very 'stamp of divinity, the nature of God, the light both of our own natural conscience and supernatural knowledge revealed.' According to Trelactius, God gives all peoples this 'revelation and gratious communication,'" said Ames.[6]

"I like your use of the image of light to explain that ectypal theology is refracted in created things," I said. "It appears that ectypal theology teaches us that God governs the world after a kind of pattern. Ectypal theology imitates the pattern. This pattern shines in all we make and design, in art and music.[7] It makes me think of 'the pattern of the tabernacle' (Exod 25:9) and 'the plan of all that he had in mind' for Solomon's Temple (1 Chr 28:11, 12), in which God's glory shone. And of Jeremiah: 'I know the plans I have for you, says the LORD, plans for your welfare and not for harm' (Jer 29:11). That 'we are what he has made us [*pŏēma*], created in Christ Jesus for good works' (Eph 2:10)—his poem, as it were," I said.

"Indeed," said Ames. "Professor Junius indicated the purpose of ectypal theology, which he said is 'the wisdom of divine matters, fashioned by God from the archetype of himself, through the communication of grace for his own glory."[8]

Commission: Ponder anew that the Son "bears the very stamp of his nature"—that is, the nature of God the Father—as "the exact imprint" (Heb 1:3), superior to the refracted imprint in created things. Also consider the heavenly pattern of the Lord's Prayer.

Matt 6:9–15; Rom 1:18–25; 2:14–15; Col 2:9–10; Heb 1:3

3

The Logos, Life, and Light

TODAY, I WENT TO Nassau Hall at what was originally the College of New Jersey (*Nova-Caesarea*), now Princeton University, to visit with Professor Geerhardus Vos (1862–1949). I asked him what the prologue to John's Gospel tells us about divine revelation and grace. Specifically, I asked whether John 1:4, 9, and 10 all refer to the beginning of time or to Jesus' birth in Bethlehem and ministry.

"I believe," said Vos, "that when John wrote in verse 1 that 'in the beginning was the Word' and in verse 4 that 'in him was life, and the life was the light of all people,' John meant to say that the role of the Logos did not begin with the birth of Jesus, who would save us from our sin. The role of the Logos reached back to creation and continued in the providence of history. The Logos has been 'supplying life and light to the natural world'—indeed, to all people—since the beginning of the world."[9]

"I take it that you do not mean to imply that the Son gave salvation to everyone in the world by saying that he was 'supplying life and light' to the world?" I asked.

"No, not at all," he said. "There is a difference between the role of the Logos as giver of light and knowledge of God in creation and in providence, and the wider, supernatural, life-giving role of the Logos as Savior of those who believe that Jesus is the resurrection and the life. But notice the order John gave to the words in the prologue when describing the meaning and role of the Logos

5

title: first 'life,' then 'light.' First, the Logos produced life, then light. 'The Genesis-account places the production of light before that of life, so that the reversed sequence in the Prologue, "In him was life, and the life (that was in him) was the light of all people," obtains a pointed significance.'[10] I recall Abraham Kuyper (1837–1920), who said, 'Christ does not come to us for the first time in the work of redemption. He is the Eternal Word, which was before all things with God and was God.'"[11]

Commission: Ponder the resurrection power of the voice of the Son, who, when he speaks, is heard by the dead.

Gen 1:3, 24, 26–27; John 1:1–18; 5:25–28

4
God's Knowledge of Approbation

I WENT TO WESTMINSTER and asked Rector Samuel Clarke (1675–1729) if God were somehow obliged to *do* what he *knows* is best and most fitting *to be done*. "Wouldn't that make sense?" I asked. "How could God do otherwise?"

"Let's begin by making a distinction between the necessity of God approving what is wise, just, and best on the one hand, and the wise, just, and best things that God actually and freely does on the other," he said. "God is a promise keeper. But, suppose God promised to destroy the world today. Is it not *possible* for God to decree a delay in the destruction? Or to not destroy at all?"

"I am confused. A promise is a promise. God must keep his promises, just as prophecies must be fulfilled some day," I said. "Furthermore, how can God go against his own best judgment?"

"I only proposed that it is *possible* for God to do otherwise than he does," said Rector Clarke.

> But not in all cases. I grant you that. But God possesses power to do as he pleases, insofar as it is consistent with his nature. Let me put it succinctly: "God always discerns and approves what is just and good, *necessarily*, and cannot do otherwise; but he always acts or does what is just and good *freely*, that is, having *at the same time* a full natural or physical power of acting differently."[12]

"Could you give me an example of a case where it is not possible for God to will otherwise than he has, with respect to our daily lives?" I asked.

"Indeed. John Duns Scotus (1266–1308) gave us ethically necessary cases wherein he argued that God cannot decree that we dishonor and hate our parents or our neighbors. Nor is it possible that God decree that we hate him with all our heart," he said.[13]

Commission: God knows best, but at the same time, God possesses the power to do otherwise; he is free to answer your prayer as he sees fit, as he pleases. You thus have every incentive to pray and petition God. God is not bound to answer one way, unless it be ethically necessary.

Pss 11:5; 115:3; Lam 3:37–66; Col 2:3

5

God's Knowledge of Simple Understanding

I met the Utrecht University professor Peter van Mastricht (1630–1706) in the academic aula. "Of all the different kinds of divine knowledge, which is the most fundamental?" I asked.

"The first of two kinds of divine knowledge that theologians wrote about, but sometimes under different names," said van Mastricht, "is what the Leiden professor Franciscus Gomarus (1563–1641) called 'the indefinite foreknowledge of God.' Professor Ames called the first 'God's knowledge of simple understanding.' The Geneva University professor Francis Turretin (1623–87) referred to the first kind as God's knowledge of simple understanding, or God's natural knowledge, or indefinite knowledge. Today I will focus on the first kind of divine knowledge."[14]

"Before you continue, could you tell me the place of God's will in relation to divine knowledge?" I asked. "And the meaning of *simple* understanding when speaking of God?"

"Those are questions of crucial importance. Generally speaking, we position the divine will *after* God's knowledge of simple understanding. It is perhaps better to explain that there is a logical, or structural, 'order of nature,' as the scholastics called it, which describes the logical relation of divine knowledge to the divine will. Of course, the term 'simple' does not carry the vulgar definition of unlearned or ignorant when speaking of God. 'Simple' refers to the perfectly complete and absolutely all-sufficient, unrestricted knowledge of God whereby God knows himself, in himself, by one pure act. God's knowledge of himself is not a composite of all his attributes. Nor does God learn things about himself by his will.

> Professor Ames said: "The knowledge of simple understanding is the most perfect knowledge in God of all possible things, that is, all things universal and particular which can be brought into being."[15]

Commission: Ponder God's pure, absolute, unconditioned, unrestricted intelligence: the knowledge whereby God knows himself does not differ from the knowledge by which he simply knows any and all possible things by his all-sufficiency. In God, "to be, to understand, to comprehend, are reciprocated. Each has recourse one to the other."[16]

Pss 90:1–2; 147:5; Matt 11:27

6

God's Knowledge of Vision

THIS LORD'S DAY, I asked Reverend Charles Morton (1627–98) at Harvard, the consumate educator at dissenter academies in England, who emigrated to Boston in 1686, to explain the second kind of divine knowledge.[17]

"I had students copy into their notebooks the following truths about the 'knowledge of vision' (*scientia visionis*)," said Morton.

> The future is known of God by knowing his own will. It is called *science of vision,* and in the order of our intellect conceiving, it is apprehended to follow his decrees, though indeed science and decrees are together eternal. It is also called free, voluntary, and definite by the circumstance of time past, present, and future.[18]

"So, God's will is crucial for all that takes place in this world, since the future that God sees is what he has willed to come to pass; no more, no less," I said. "Unlike God, 'we walk by faith, not by sight' (2 Cor 5:7). I also take note again of the function of the conceptual notion 'the order of our intellect,' by which you have positioned the *knowledge of vision* after the decree of the will."[19]

"Yes, but this *order* is purely for teaching purposes, since God's decrees and knowledge are both eternal—that is, outside time," said Reverend Morton.

Now let's put it all together: "Hence the schoolmen conceive all things as in a twofold estate of possibility and fruition. Between those two they place the act of God's will to transfer a thing from the act of possibility to a state of futurition, God knows both, say they, the one antecedently to the will and the other consequently."[20]

"It appears that God's will, then, is the hinge, as it were, between the two kinds of knowledge. Is God obliged to transfer all possible things that he knows into the realm of futurity?" I asked.

"Absolutely not. For then all things would be necessary. But God is not omnivolent," he said.[21]

Commission: God sees you in your circumstances as sure as he has willed the sun to rise and set on your household, and the seasons to come and go, all according to the council of his good will.

Gen 16:13; Hab 2:2–3; Matt 6:4; Acts 15:18; 2 Cor 5:7

7

God's Negative Indifference

TODAY, I ASKED LEIDEN professor Adriaan Heereboord (1614–61) to explain the subtle nuances that attend *negative indifference* and if God were ever indifferent.[22]

"Would it not be better to speak of God's neutrality in the face of decisions?" I suggested.

"No. For there are acts of God that are negative, such as with respect to sin; they are not merely neutral. By not softening the heart, or not positively hardening the heart of Pharaoh, God is negatively indifferent with respect to the cause of sin. God will not coerce anyone to love and obey him. Now, God, with respect to who he is in himself, is indifferent to the possibility of works outside himself. God's essential attributes—his grace, goodness, and all-sufficiency—make God no more determined to create than not to create," he said.

"But wasn't God always going to manifest his creative powers and create this world?" I asked. "In the end, God couldn't hold back from exercising his powers, could he?"

"I notice that you used the adverb *always*. But your use of *always* implied a kind of necessity, as if it were necessary, 'in the end,' that God create. The other uses of the adverb *always* refer to time. And this is the point I want to make. I want you to think outside the boundaries of time. It is difficult for us, as humans, to conceive of a negative indifference in God's mind that is outside of time. But I am asking you to place God's negative indifference prior to the will of God to create the world. To do this requires the use of the conceptual tool we call *signum rationis*. The term speaks of a logical or structural order, whereby we can position our talk about negative indifference. God, in the essence of his nature, was indifferent to creating or not creating, or even to creating another kind of world than this one. Nothing determined God's will one way or the other," he said.[23]

Commission: Ponder the notion that negative indifference implies no imperfection, privation, or indecisiveness in God. Ultimately, God negatively, without coercion, leaves people to harden their own hearts. God cannot be charged with being the author or actor of evil in this world.

Exod 9:12; 14:17; 1 Sam 2:25; Eph 1:4; 2 Tim 2:19; Rev 4:11

8

God's Double Glory

THIS LORD'S DAY, I encountered the English Congregational divine Thomas Goodwin (1600–80). He made a distinction between God's "essential glory" and his "manifestative glory."[24]

I asked him, "What moved God to manifest his glory to us that we might praise his essential grace and goodness, and the glory of his grace?"

"First and foremost," Dr. Goodwin said, "there is a difference between God's goodness and grace in and of themselves on the one hand, and the praise of God's goodness and grace on the other. The first truth belongs to God essentially, whether any person—including angels—is formed and praises the glory of God's attributes, or not. Were God never to create anything, this truth would stand for eternity. The second truth gets to the heart of your question. What moved God was his love, which saw fit to have his will go forth to choose us in Christ the Son and predestine us to praise God's glory."

"You have spoken of the principle '*bonum est sui diffusivum*, all goodness is communicative of itself, so glory is manifestive of itself.'[25] Could you explain if God was somehow necessitated to communicate his goodness and grace to us?" I asked.

"There is a distinction to be made," he said, "between the eternally necessary action of the Father begetting the Son in the Trinity on the one hand, and God the Father freely choosing and electing us in the Son on the other, with the purpose that we praise the glory of his grace. Since God is a communicative Being, love moves him to manifest his glory. Nevertheless, to answer your question, remember that unlike what belongs to God *essentially*, his *manifestative glory* only belongs to him in a relative sense. Perhaps it must remain a mystery, but God's love for his glory to be praised moved him, 'yet not so but that he could have done otherwise, he needed not to have cared for it.'"[26]

Commission: Ponder carefully the opening verses that Paul wrote to the Ephesians, pausing at every comma, in order to get the correct sense of the passage to understand what belongs to God's essential glory and what belongs to his manifestative glory.

Matt 11:26; Eph 1:3–6

9

God's Double Plotline

THIS LORD'S DAY, I met with Jonathan Edwards at his home in Stockbridge. He was intrigued by God's double plotline as explained by Thomas Goodwin in his *Exposition of Ephesians*.[27]

"Goodwin," Edwards said, "told us that the primary story line of God the Father was the romance and marriage of an exalted royal couple. From eternity past, the Father sought to procure a spouse for his Son. The secondary plotline saw his 'espoused love' get into trouble, misfortunes, and hardships, throwing her into 'sin and misery.' But God 'sends his Son Jesus Christ to rescue her.' The 'plot of redemption' was a second edition, as it were, of the love of God and of Christ."[28]

"I take it that the royal couple is Christ the Son and his spouse, the church," I said.

"Indeed, and do you know what God's purpose was through the misery?" he asked. "It was, Goodwin wrote, 'to take our hearts the more when we shall come to see his person in heaven.'"[29]

"Have you written about this double plotline in your '*Miscellanies*' notebooks?" I asked.

"Indeed. I wrote that 'Christ is first in this affair, and the ground of our being chosen.' The Son is 'the end of all God's works *ad extra*.' The 'sum' of God's purposes 'with respect to creatures, was to procure a spouse, or a mystical body, for his Son.' Think of it—you and I were chosen to be members of the elect spouse herself, 'for the adequate displays of his unspeakable and transcendent goodness and grace.' All together 'in one body, one spouse, all united in one head.' There are christological remarks that I also have made," he said. "Consider that 'the man Christ Jesus is first of the elect,' the fruit of free, sovereign election. A super-creation—a proleptic view of Christ as God-man, to be incarnated (*incarnandus*). But 'God's love to the eternal *Logos* itself is not by sovereign election, but by merit and natural necessity in the highest degree.'"[30]

Commission: Ponder God's purpose in all his works *ad extra* to procure a spouse for his Son—namely, Christ as God-man (*incarnandus*). God's sovereign good pleasure was the only reason, as Jonathan Edwards reasoned, why God chose one person to be a member of the elect spouse, the church, and not another.

Rom 5:8; Eph 1:4, 9–10

10

God's Double Gift

I WANTED TO FOLLOW up last Lord's Day exercises, and so I visited with Thomas Goodwin and asked him about what he calls "the double gift of Christ to us and for us."[31]

Goodwin began by asking me a question: "Which is the least of the two—the gift of Christ as our Redeemer, or the gift of Christ himself?" he asked. "If that is too difficult, let me ask you another way: 'Tell me whether dost thou prize more the person of Jesus Christ given thee, or the benefits thou hast by his death.'"[32]

"For the first question, I had never thought of it that way, but I see that I first choose Christ himself for who he is, not for what he has done for me. And to the second, I answer that I prize the person of Christ most."

"You answered well. For I always say 'that Christ's love for us is more than his sufferings; his sufferings worth more than all his benefits; but his person is more than either benefits or sufferings.'[33] When God chose you in Christ and accepted you as a son or a daughter to live and commune with him, that was God's first intended gift to you. Christ given *to* you. Then, over and above this, God gave Christ as Redeemer *for* you."

"I see how great a theological point can be made by changing one preposition," I said.

"Let me go further and ask you to ponder this:

Est aliquid in Christo formosius salvatore—There is something in Christ more beautiful, more amiable and glorious, than his being a Saviour.[34]

"Let me ask you: Is not Christ 'God's beloved' in whom he delights, whom he loves, and 'not for any benefit of redemption by him'? The Son is '*primum amabile*, loved for himself; and so let him be to thee.'"[35]

Commission: Discern the distinction between being "blessed in the Beloved" purely for who he is, and the benefit of being accepted by him, "in whom we have redemption through his blood" (Eph 1:7).

Prov 8:30; Song 1:16; Matt 3:17; Eph 1:6–7

11

God's Physical Influx

THIS LORD'S DAY, I once again spent time with Professor Peter van Mastricht. I wanted to understand the meaning of the confusing term "physical" in scholastic Latin—a word which I often read in expressions such as "physical premotion," "physical predetermination," and, in today's disputation, both a physical and a predetermining influx in the affairs of people.

"Very often," said Van Mastricht, "students are asked to prepare a response to the following question: 'Whether there is such an influx of divine providence, by which God physically predetermines all causes, by all means, to act?'[36] Students usually begin with the Scripture passage 'In him we live and move and have our being' (Acts 17:28) in order to establish our dependence upon God, who moves upon and quickens our soul's faculties," he said.

"But doesn't a physical predetermination imply that God's sovereign providence violates our individual freedom, and worse yet, makes God the author of our sinful acts?" I asked.

"Not at all," replied Van Mastricht. "In fact, that is usually the second question paired with the first. The student debates this question: 'Whether the predetermining influx makes God the author of sin?'[37] The student would answer in the negative. First, evil is not a positive thing that exists and upon which God can operate. Evil is the absence of good; it marks a deficiency in you and me. Second, and crucially, there is a distinction between the physical-substrate level of reality, the level upon which God works and moves in this world, on the one hand, and the moral level of your acts and mine on the other. The moral dimension belongs inherently to you and me. Therefore, God is not to be held accountable for the morality of our acts of the will. Nor can sin, therefore, be traced back to God's *physical* predetermining influx. For it is not a moral influx."

Commission: Although "in him we live and move and have our being" (Acts 17:28) and he is the one who moves upon our souls, virtue and vice belong to us, not God. If we ask, as Van Mastricht did, "Whether or not divine providence may sometimes result in sin?"[38] we should recall that God may will to permit sin, which is a neutral permission, or may withold the grace of softening a heart, as in the case of Pharaoh. Thus, God is not caught up in sin.

Exod 10:1; Ps 104:19–20, 29; Acts 17:28

12

God's Passions and Immutability 1

THIS LORD'S DAY, I met with the Presbyterian divine and pastor Stephen Charnock (1628–80) at Crosby Hall, London, where he was teaching a series on the existence and attributes of God. I asked him about a troubling thought many have—whether God ever repents and changes his mind, and if so, how does he remain immutable?

"We read of 'if, then' propositions, such as 'If that nation, concerning which I have spoken, turns from its evil, I will change my mind about the disaster that I intended to bring on it' (Jer 18:8). But properly speaking, God does not repent, since to repent implies something unforeseen by God, which then implies God's ignorance. Nor is grief, properly speaking, to be found in God, though we read in Genesis 6:6 that 'the LORD was sorry that he had made humankind on the earth, and it grieved him to his heart.' Let me illustrate. Does the sun change when it melts wax? Or brings out a flower's fragrance, or makes a dead carcass stink? No. Likewise, God is pure Spirit and thus not capable of mood swings; he is not weak and vulnerable, as we are. Human grief is not compatible with God, who is forever blessed. Here is the key. The cause of grief and repentance is not in the sun, which changes not, but in the disposition and heart of the subject," he said.[39]

"What we read in Scripture," he said, "is the language of accommodation. God accommodates himself to us. After all, God has no body. He has no passion or anger, as we do. He is never visibly shaken. You see, God clothes himself with the language of human nature, that we might begin to understand him. Crucially, repentance in God is merely a change in how he acts outwardly toward us. In himself, God always hates the bad and always loves the good."

Commission: Sometimes we see God's righteous anger, sometimes his loving-kindness. But God hasn't changed. When we repent, we express grief for past conduct and ask for grace to change going forward. 'But God does not repent *in time* of what he did not repent *from eternity*.'[40] In other words, the wickedness that God sees play out in time, such as in Genesis 6, does not catch God by surprise. In himself, in eternity past—thus, outside of time—God has repented and it has grieved him to his heart.

Gen 6:5–8; Jer 18:7–12; John 4:24; Rom 9:5; Jas 1:17

13

God's Passions and Immutability 2

THERE REMAINED SO MANY questions in my mind about whether God has passions, that I returned to Crosby Hall, London, to pick up where we had left off with Pastor Stephen Charnock. I asked him if the positions taken on this topic by the Thirty-Nine Articles of the Church of England, 1571, and the Westminster Confession of Faith, 1647, shed any more light on the subject.

"The Church of England, article 1," said Charnock, "states, 'There is but one living and true God, everlasting, without body, parts, or passions [*impassibilis*].'[41] The Westminster Confession is almost the same. Chapter 2.1 says, 'There is but one only living and true God, who is infinite in being and perfection, a most pure spirit, invisible, without body, parts, or passions [*sine passionibus*], immutable.'[42] Unlike human beings or the gods of mythology, God does not suffer from lust, anxiety, or fear."

"Which Scripture passages do the framers of the Confession give in support of impassibility?" I asked.

"The Westminster divines gave an interesting Scripture passage to explain impassibility: Acts 14:11–15. When Paul and Barnabas were at Lystra, they healed a crippled man, and the crowds shouted, 'The gods have come down to us in human form!' They called Barnabas Zeus, Paul Hermes. But Barnabas and Paul cried out, 'We also are men of like passions with you' (Acts 14:15 KJV). In other words, human beings share human nature in common and thus cannot be gods, or the one true God, as Barnabas and Paul certainly would have been thinking. For God does not have *passions*, as men do. God's nature is unlike ours. Though God's promises and threats may appear to go unfulfilled in Scripture, and imply a change in God's will, there is no change in God. The change is in the person. For instance, when God gave Hezekiah a reprieve from death, and when God reversed course with Nineveh," he said.[43]

Commission: In covenantal promises, God fulfills his promises when the other party performs the demands. But in covenantal threats, the obligation to obey is upon the sinner. God has the right to punish or to extend grace. In this, his initial will changes not.

2 Kgs 20:1–11; Isa 38:1–5; Nah 1:1–3; Mal 3:6; Acts 14:11–15

14

Christ Our Surety

THIS LORD'S DAY, I asked Pastor Charnock how God could relax his own law while honoring his attributes. Would God not in effect be dishonoring his attributes of justice and righteousness?

"No, not at all. Here's why. Though God's will is to declare the demerit of sin," answered Charnock, "God transfers the punishment from the offender to a Person substituted in his place—as with Adam and Eve, who did not immediately die upon disobedience to their Creator—a Surety in the place of the malefactor. Likewise, as in the case of a nation that turns from evil, God removes the intended punishment from the table and lets mercy flow. In these cases, God upholds and honors his attributes by interposing a Mediator. God grounds this action of grace upon the work of Jesus Christ, our Surety. But the universal rule remains intact—namely, that if a nation or an individual persists in evil and warnings are ignored, judgment will come."[44]

"So, what about predictions—even promises—in the Scriptures of good and welfare that will come to us? Are they not absolute?" I asked.

"Not at all," he said. "'Absolute' means unconditional, unrestricted, unconnected. If you recall your grammar, an absolute phrase bears an unrestricted relation to the rest of the sentence. Thus, if a nation returns to its past evil ways, or if the next generation rejects the faith of its parents and does not repent or call upon the Mediator, all predictions of welfare are off the table. 'When God threatened Nineveh, they were a fit object for justice. But when they repented they were a fit object for mercy.'"[45]

Commission: The good news is that the natural notion that all people have of God's goodness and mercy as established in Scripture affords hope of relief. If they heed God's prophetic call, "humble themselves, pray, seek [God's] face, and turn from their wicked ways, then [he] will hear from heaven and forgive their sin and heal their land" (2 Chr 7:14), all made possible thanks to the Surety, the Mediator, Jesus Christ, to whom God has transferred the debt of the offender's sin.

2 Chr 7:14; Ezek 18:20–21; Jonah 3:4–10; Heb 7:22; 9:15

15

God's Foreknowledge and Human Freedom

THIS LORD'S DAY, BEFORE leaving Crosby Hall, London, I wanted to ask Pastor Charnock to explain why God's foreknowledge of our choices in life does not necessitate our will and action. If God knows everything, are we truly free? My hunch was that since God acts freely, so do we.

"First, be assured that God's foreknowledge of our human activity does not increase or grow, nor can God be caught unawares or deceived by what we do," said Pastor Charnock. "Second, we must understand the different nuances of *necessity*. If God were to receive counsel or guidance from himself that compels, guides, or directs him, he indeed would not be free. This is a 'compulsive necessity.'[46] But the fact that God is necessarily immutable does not remove his liberty. Nor does the fact that God is necessarily infallible remove his liberty. Nor does God's infallible foreknowledge violate our liberty. God cannot *not* be essentially holy, good, and infallible. Yet is he free. God in himself freely, without compulsion, decreed that he would create the world. And so God's work outside himself was free. He freely created the world."

"Now I understand Paul's rhetorical question 'Who hath been his counsellor?' (Rom 11:34 KJV)."

"Think about it," said Pastor Charnock. "'Who hath been God's compeller?' No one. Moreover, although the Son 'necessarily took our flesh, because he had covenanted with God to do so,' our Lord Jesus acted freely, saying, 'I lay down my life of my own accord' (John 10:18).[47] Was the prophecy about the bones of Christ (John 19:36) necessary in eternity prior to the prophecy?"

"No," I said. "Normally, in fact, necessarily, bones are inherently breakable, not unbreakable."

"Exactly," he replied. "Thus, the unbreakability of the bones of Christ was contingent upon the prophecy, and therefore, not a hard kind of necessity. Nevertheless, the prophecy would be fulfilled infallibly. You see, therefore, how infallibility can be so easily misunderstood as not compatible with liberty."

Commission: Ponder the compatibility of God's infallible foreknowledge of Jesus' covenant obedience with Jesus' liberty in laying down his life for us.

Ps 40:6–8; John 8:29; 10:17–18; 12:49; 19:36; Phil 2:5–11

16

The Will: Producible versus Produced

I STILL HAD QUESTIONS about the compatibility of infallibility and liberty, so I visited with Lord Archbishop John Bramhall (1594-1663), an Anglican from Ardmagh, Ireland. The marquis of Newcastle had arranged a meeting in 1645 between the bishop and the English philosopher Thomas Hobbes (1588-1679) while the marquis was in exile in Paris. I heard that quite a controversy about liberty and necessity ensued, with an exchange of treatises. I asked the bishop to explain to me how our wills are truly "masters of our own acts."[48]

"The will, both God's and ours, is a self-determining power. But there is a distinction to be made between the power of the will to produce an effect (producibility) and the produced effect (production). Hobbes conflates what should be held distinct. But unless you and I are restrained or otherwise physically hindered, we are free agents and retain the possibility (power) not to will to produce an effect at the moment when, in fact, we do will it. In other words, you and I *can* forbear to will to love someone, even when we will to love. Otherwise, we are not free to love. I don't want to imagine a world without true freedom to obey God's command to love him and others. Unfortunately, Hobbes holds that 'the will is necessitated extrinsically to every act of willing.' His example is of a river descending down a channel."[49]

"But isn't there a contradiction in saying that I can will to love and forbear to love at the same time?" I asked.

"If we are careless with our words," he said, "simultaneously willing to love and forbearing to love the same person is indeed a contradiction. But, 'in the same instant wherein the will elects, it is free, according to a priority of nature, though not of time, to elect otherwise. And so in a divided sense, the will is free, even whilst it acts.'[50] Next Lord's Day, I will explain the meaning of 'priority of nature' versus 'time' and the meaning of the 'divided sense,'" he said.

Commission: Thankfully, the world God created is not one in which he compels or coerces us against our will to love him, our spouse, our children, our grandchildren, or our neighbor. There would be no virtue on our part if this were called "love," which indeed is not God's design of love at all.

Deut 6:4–15; Jer 31:1–3, 18–22; Hos 4:17; John 3:16–21

17

The Priority of Nature versus Time

"TODAY, I WILL CLARIFY what I mean by 'the priority of nature' and 'the divided sense' of a proposition," said Bishop Bramhall. "For there is a 'fallacy of division,' if misunderstood."[51]

"I remember Professor Adriaan Heereboord speaking about the conceptual device which he called a logical, or structural, 'order of nature' (*signum rationis*), not of time, which he paired with his teaching about God's *negative indifference*," I said.[52]

"Indeed," said the Bishop. "Recall what Jesus said: 'The blind see' (Luke 7:22). If it were not Jesus speaking, you might disagree. But, when I divide the proposition with a comma, the sense can be as follows: *Though once I was blind, now I see*. The divided sense separating the parts gives a diachronic reading—from a past status of blindness to a present moment of sight. Now let us unfold the mystery further. Suppose I read the divided sense of the proposition apart from two separate moments of time. Then it reads, and means, *Though I am blind, it is possible that I see, in the same instant*. The alternative possibility of sight is read in a synchronic sense of simultaneity rather than a diachronic sense, and is logically possible. If read in a compound sense, it would end in a contradiction, since, indeed, the blind do not see. So, the priority of nature is a purely conceptual way of giving priority to a *free* will, above and beyond, as it were, the instant I will to do something or not to do something. In this way, we can speak about *before* and *after* the act of the will without referring to real moments of time."[53]

"So, there is an *order of nature* and an *order of time*. The former is nontemporal," I said.

"Precisely. These are very common terms of art. And crucially, in the order of nature, we assign 'dominion over our own acts, to will or nill without extrinsical necessitation.'[54] Give me time, a pen, ink, paper, and a desk, and I am free to write further on this matter for you. But whether I actually do or not is a distinction we must maintain," said the bishop.

Commission: Assign to God the sovereign priority of the divine will outside time and according to the *priority of nature*, and you will see that God is ever present to our willing and choosing. For God is at work in you, both to will and to work for his good pleasure.

Matt 11:4–6; Mark 1:40–41; Rom 4:5; Phil 2:13

18

The Noble Cause

BEFORE LEAVING IRELAND, I spent another Lord's Day with Bishop Bramhall to ask him how it is that, if God is the first cause in a so-called chain of necessary secondary causes—a chain that not even Jove could break—our world and our choices are contingent and free, not necessitated.

"The rule of propositions," he said, "is that 'no effect can exceed the virtue of its cause. If the ability or debility, of the causes be contingent, the effect cannot be necessary.'[55] "Leiden professor Franco Burgersdijk (1590–1635) said that 'the principle cause is either equal to or nobler than the effect.'"[56]

"It seems to me, then, that if the first cause in the 'sequence' is necessary, then this necessity transfers to all the subsequent causes. Likewise, if the first cause is free, then the subsequent causes must be free and contingent," I said. "They cannot be necessary if the first cause is not."

"Precisely. Franciscans like Duns Scotus argued that there is contingency in the things of this world, and that God's will is the root source of all contingency.[57] Thus, God, as the first cause, freely imparts, as it were, the power needed for natural causes and other secondary causes, like you and me, to do what they and we do. Consequently, the contingency of effects is grounded in God's freedom," he said. "In fact, God's freedom entails the possibility to alter the cause-effect relation so that certain causes, like the laws of nature, for instance, do not produce their effects."

"Do you and I, as secondary agents, need to concur with God in producing the effect that he wills to be brought about through us?" I asked.

"Excellent question. There are differences of opinion. If our concurring in a matter were not taken into account and there were no real alternative possibilities of choice for God or for us at every moment, then our lives would be necessitated, and we would live in a fatally determined world. But there is a concurrence, even a priority, of God's will as first cause and our will as secondary cause."[58]

Commission: Here is a mystery. God's will empowers our faculties but in no way violates our freedom of will; rather, he preserves it. God's love freely moves our soul as his beloved.

Job 12:10; Ps 87:7; 1 John 4:7–12

19

The Soul's Power of the Will

THIS LORD'S DAY, I found myself once again at Crosby Hall with Pastor Stephen Charnock. I wanted to get his opinion on the soul's power of the will to do otherwise than it in fact does.

"Let me begin with a statement that may shock you," he said. "'Man hath a power to do otherwise than that which God foreknows he will do.'"[59]

"I must say, when I hear that, it appears to state that God is ignorant of our actions. But you must mean that while God foreknows future, contingent human actions, humans, nevertheless, possess the power to act otherwise than they in fact do," I said.

"God knows both our actual action and the possible alternatives. As God's will concurs with ours, he also possesses the power to do otherwise than he in fact does. But God does not coerce us. 'When a man writes or speaks, whilst he writes or speaks, those actions are necessary, because to speak and be silent, to write and not to write, at the same time, are impossible. Our writing or speaking does not take away the power not to write or to be silent at that time if a man would be so; for he might have chosen whether he would have spoken or written.'"[60]

"Now, God necessarily foresees our actions, but what kind of necessity is it?" I asked.

"You ask well. We call this a 'necessity of infallibility.' Remember, no choice or circumstance can surprise God. But this kind of necessity does not compel or coerce anyone. God foresees when we will eat, work, love, play, petition him in prayer, or sleep. You recall Adam in Eden? Even Adam did not blame God as if he had compelled him to eat the forbidden fruit. He blamed Eve. Adam never thought of the charges that future generations would concoct to blame God for their misdeeds. Nor did Judas charge Jesus' foreknowledge with his betrayal of our Lord. Judas freely did what he did, and therefore repented of it. Nor did Peter blame Jesus for foretelling that Peter would thrice deny him. Peter owned his denials."

Commission: There is no blind necessity coercing you to do what you do. Don't believe it for a second. Discard the ancient proverb "The fathers have eaten sour grapes, and the children's teeth are set on edge" (Jer 31:29). Each individual soul belongs to the Lord, and to him are you accountable.

Gen 3:8–13; Ezek 18:1–32; Luke 22:34, 54–62; John 13:21–26; Rom 5:12–17

20

Shipwrecked and God's Physical Predetermination 1

ALTHOUGH I SIDED WITH Bishop Bramhall in his debate with Hobbes for freedom against fatalism, I wasn't entirely satisfied with Bishop Bramhall's answers. Nor were Pastor Charnock's explanations enough. I recalled Professor Van Mastricht's distinction between the nonmoral *physical* dimension of God acting upon our faculties in the reality of this world and the *moral* dimension and responsibility of our actions. To satisfy my inquiring mind, I visited Samuel Rutherford (1600–1661), rector of the University of St Andrews in Scotland.

"Essentially, you are asking me if my will concurs with God's, or if God's will concurs with mine, or if there is a simultaneous concurrence of wills," Rector Rutherford said. "First, recall that our soul's faculties cannot declare independence from God. We cannot produce any effect without God's concurrence and empowerment of our faculties. Second, God ordains the secondary means—that is where you, and I, and the natural realm come in—as well as the end, thereby securing *his* desired outcome, yet without violating our mastery over our own wills, nor succumbing to the forces of nature, nor being caught off guard by the supposed unpredicatability of human action."[61]

"But in the case of Saint Paul's shipwreck (Acts 27), it seems as if fate and Mother Nature determined whether the ship, the cargo, the crew, Paul, and the other prisoners were to arrive safely in Italy, not God," I said. "Did not God have to concur with secondary causes?"[62]

"Not at all. God was not forced to oblige fate, nor fortune, nor the northeaster, nor the crew's choices to jettison cargo and such. God taught Paul a lesson in divine providence. God's willing and movement were immediately present in the northeaster, the crew's decisions, the centurion's decision, and Paul's decision on the *physical* level of reality. In the night, an angel of God had assured Paul that he and all 276 persons on the ship would survive the voyage. Thus, even though the soldiers had planned to kill the prisoners after striking a reef, the centurion scuttled their plan. Yet, who would say that the centurion and Paul were just puppets in God's plan, and that they were not free?"

Commission: You do not know what tomorrow will bring. Make a habit of declaring, "If the Lord wills, we will live and do this or that" (Jas 4:15) rather than "If I will, the Lord will concur with me."

Prov 16:9; 27:1; Acts 27:1–44; Jas 4:13–15

21

Shipwrecked and God's Physical Predetermination 2

I REMAINED AT ST Andrews and requested more time with Rector Rutherford. I asked him to explain the *pre* in predetermination and why he does not find a general concurrence acceptable.

"One major objective I have is that God's influx and moving upon our faculties really is a cause, a *pre*determining influx, and thus precedes our choice," said Rector Rutherford.

"But would that not violate our freedom and make God the author of sin?" I asked.

"No. Think about it. If, as some claim, God's influx in our lives follows our choices, then the consequence is that we humans determine God's knowledge of our actions. Moreover, it would imply the unthinkable—namely, that God merely concurs with our choices," he said. "We, as secondary causes, do not predetermine God's choices, for he is the primary cause, not us."[63]

"Recalling the example from last Lord's Day of Paul's shipwreck, wouldn't God merely concur with secondary causes, such as natural causes, northeasters, tides, trade winds, and so forth?" I asked.

"Indeed. But note the difference between God's concurrence with the cause and effect of winds, tides, and fire that burns, and the 'justice' of venomous snake bites, such as Paul had on the island of Malta. The human soul is not to be compared with all these examples from nature. Fire burns. That is what fire does. But not so with human choice and the virtue or vice of human action. But in the case of Paul's venomous snakebite, God showed that he can, if he so wills, intervene and overrule the normal deadly course of venom running in Paul's veins. Recall the centurion's decision to keep Paul and all prisoners safe. There is virtue associated with sparing human life, thanks to God's commands and Paul's reminder to the centurion and crew. Although God *predetermined* the centurion's decision to spare lives, the immediacy of God's move on his soul as he decided is not prior in time but in the causal priority, or order of nature. But it is the centurion's will that actually produced the moral, and thus virtuous, effect."[64]

Commission: Imitate Paul's assurance and faith in God's providence—not in fate, in fortune, or in "justice"—that all persons would be spared, that the centurion would make the right decision, and that Paul would arrive safely in Italy. Remember that "we walk by faith, not by sight" (2 Cor 5:7).

Acts 27:43–28:6; 2 Cor 5:7; Heb 11:1

22

Prayer for Such a Time as This

Rector Rutherford and I picked up where we had left off last Lord's Day at St Andrews. I was intrigued by God's providence in history and asked him about Queen Esther's prayer.

"You may recall last week that we talked about the *immediacy* of God's presence to our actions. This is a crucial concept to wrap our minds around in order to understand why Esther's prayer mattered. The fate of the Jewish people did not rest upon Esther alone. Nor did it rest upon God alone. And crucially, nor did it rest upon some kind of simultaneous agreement and concurrence by God with Esther's prayer. God did not accommodate his plans to her wishes. Nor did Esther somehow bind God morally with her petition," said Rector Rutherford.

"You have said what Esther's prayer could not do, always negatively. But positively, what did it accomplish?" I asked. "Why did her prayer matter?"

"First, I wanted to remove the dangerous opinions that would lead us to conclude either that God can only wait for Esther to pray and then react to her prayer, or that God clearly has limitations and imperfections and cannot save the Jewish people without her, or that God must coerce her to cooperate, or that God doesn't really need her at all and can do it alone. But while Esther's prayer matters, so does the immediacy of God's previous influx on the *physical* level of her soul to quicken her prayer so that she request the one thing that God himself has *predetermined* and planned to do—namely, to rescue her people. The mystery is in how God guarded not only her freedom to choose to enter the king's court and make her petition, but also the king's freedom to hold out the golden scepter or not. God empowered both in the physical dimension and reality of their souls—for Esther to fast and pray, and for King Ahasuerus to grant her petition—with God's immediate presence active in both."[65]

Commission: Ponder God's providence in the words and actions of Mordecai, Esther, and King Ahasuerus (Xerxes). Mordecai's "Who knows?" (Esth 4:15) expresses his and Esther's hope in God's providential power to move the heart of the king so that she find favor in his eyes and he grant her petition.

Esth 3:13–5:3; Job 23:10–17; Prov 21:1; Jas 5:16–18

23

Christian Fate

ALTHOUGH I HAD LEFT Rector Rutherford at St Andrews, I spoke with the Swiss pastor and divine Johann Friedrich Stapfer (1708–75) about the different kinds of fate of which both he and Rector Rutherford had written, including what they called "Christian fate."[66]

"Does it surprise you to hear Rector Rutherford and I speak about Christian fate?" Pastor Stapfer asked. "There is yet another kind of fate of which Rector Rutherford could not know: the fate held by Baruch Spinoza (1632–77). But first, there is 'Stoic fate,' which holds to the necessity of all things that happen in this world, due to the divine decrees. Stoic fate denies that you and I act freely. It also denies the contingency of things that happen in this world—that is, that things could be otherwise than they are. Second, 'Islamic fate' excludes both means and motives. That means that both your action and mine are meaningless to God in the end. God's will shall be accomplished with or without our prayers, petitions, or fasting, or even any natural causes and means. Third, 'Spinozoan fate' subordinates all means to the end—means such as prayer, fasting, preaching, prophecy, harbingers. It excludes any kind of contingency from the world," he said.[67]

"What, then, is Christian fate?" I asked.

"If by 'fate' we mean nothing other than to stress the certainty of future events—that prophecy will be fulfilled, that our hope in the return of Jesus the Messiah is real, not empty, that we are content to rest in God's providential care—then yes, there is such a thing as Christian fate. Do you know what *fatum* means? Gottfried Wilhelm Leibniz (1646–1716) pointed out that *fatum* is derived from *fari*, which means 'to decree,' as in, God's providential decree.[68] Recall Gen 1:3: 'Then God said, "Let there be light."' There was no one to hear God's voice, no one to petition him, but his powerful voice freely and authoritatively produced light out of a formless void and darkness. If that is not a decree, I know not what is."

Commission: Exercise the patience of Job to rest in and be content with God's providence, but not to the neglect of petitioning him and casting your cares upon him, for he does care for you (1 Pet 5:7).

Gen 1:1–3; Job 9:32–33; 13:3, 15; 16:18–22; Rom 8:28; Heb 11:3; Jas 5:11

24

Sifting Providence Down to the Pure Bran 1

THIS LORD'S DAY, I spoke at length with John Dryden (1631–1700) about his adaptation of "The Nun's Priest's Tale" by Geoffrey Chaucer (1343–1400).

Dryden said, "Both Chaucer and I crafted our verse to address the issue of God's prescience and whether God is the author of sin. For instance, I wrote, 'Some clerks [scholars] maintain that heaven at first foresees, / And in the virtue of foresight decrees. / If this be so, then prescience binds the will, / And mortals are not free to good or ill; / For what he first foresaw, he must ordain, / Or its eternal prescience may be in vain; / As bad for us as prescience had not been; / For, first or last, he's author of the sin.'"[69]

"I see the problem of placing God's prescience of our action before the decree. If God reacts and speaks his decrees based first on what he sees you and I doing, then it seems as if you and I dictate to God what he must decree. His own prescience, as you say, would bind his own will. This would land us in a necessitated and fated world of our own making, would it not?" I said.

"Indeed it would," said Dryden. "Nor do I see how God could punish vice or reward virtue, especially if prescience comes first. As I wrote, 'I cannot bolt this matter to the bran, / As Bradwardine and holy Austin [Augustine] can.' One thing I know is that we are 'not forced to sin by strict necessity; / This strict necessity they simple call, / Another sort there is conditional.' Simple necessity is absolute and binds the will. Conditional necessity does not constrain freedom. Absolute necessity implies that God foresees human action as no different than that of animals doing what they are designed to do: 'Thus galley slaves tug willing at their oar, / Consent to work, in prospect of the shore— / But would not work at all, if not constrained before.' But humans can act or refrain from acting: 'Heaven made us agents free to good or ill, / And forced it not, though he foresaw the will. / Freedom was first bestowed on human race, / And prescience only held the second place.'"[70]

Commission: Note the English poet John Dryden's awe: "If he [God] could make such agents wholly free, / I do not dispute: the point's too high for me; / For heaven's unfathomed power what man can sound, / Or put to his omnipotence a bound?"[71]

Job 42:1–6; Pss 131: 1–3; 139:1–18; Isa 55:6–9

25

Sifting Providence Down to the Pure Bran 2

THIS LORD'S DAY, I talked with Geoffrey Chaucer about "The Nun's Priest's Tale" from *The Canterbury Tales*, which had inspired John Dryden's tale. I asked him about the verse "Or elles, if free choys be graunted me / To do that same thyng, or do it noght, / Though God forwoot it er that I was wroght; / Or of his wityng streyneth never a deel / But by necessitee condicioneel"[72]—which has been translated today as "Or whether a free choice is granted me, / To do it or not do it, either one, / Though God must know all things before they are done; / Or whether his foresight nowise can constrain / Except contingently, as some explain."[73]

"First, let me explain," said Chaucer, "that it is difficult to sift out the good arguments from the bad on both sides of the argument. My verse gives high regard to Saint Augustine, bishop of Hippo (354–430), Boethius (ca. 475–526), and Thomas Bradwardine, archbishop of Canterbury (ca. 1290–1349), all of whom can 'bolt it to the husks'—that is, 'sift the arguments down to the pure bran.'[74] Second, I borrowed the phrase 'by necessitee condicioneel' from my translation of Boethius's *De Consolatione Philosophiae* and from Bradwardine's *De Causa Dei*."[75]

"Bradwardine used the term 'conditional necessity,'" I said, "to mean an 'inferential necessity'—that is, there is a mere inference in the necessity of the consequence of God's decree and foreknowledge

49

of what he has decreed. For instance, Boethius said, 'Necessarily, if you know that a man is walking, then he is walking.'[76] Or, if I am married, then I have a spouse. But there is no absolute necessity that a man be walking, nor that I be married."

"Indeed. Boethius's point was that God's foreknowledge of our actions does not necessitate our actions," said Chaucer. "God's foreknowledge, as you say, is a mere necessity of the consequence of the proposition 'Necessarily, God knows and foresees what he decrees.'"

Commission: Ponder how God's certain knowledge of all our contingency plans, as we often call them, in no way violates our freedom to plan or act; but always say, "Your will be done."

1 Sam 23:1–14; Matt 6:9–15; 26:31–75

26

Sifting Providence Down to the Pure Bran 3

BEFORE LEAVING THE PEOPLE of Chaucer's fourteenth-century England, I wanted to ask him about the tragedy of fate in his *Troilus and Criseyde*.

"It appears," I said, "that Troilus had difficulty reconciling God's eternal prescience with his own free choice in this love story. As a storyteller, you wanted us to feel his frustration. But, as in the 'Nun's Priest's Tale,' you were meditating on Boethius's *De Consolatione Philosophiae* again, and as a greedy miser, you mined what you could as you puzzled over divine 'purveyaunce' (providence) and 'fre chois' (free choice) through this character."[77]

Chaucer said, "Yes, Troilus discerned that the 'forsight of divine purveyaunce' had disposed that he would have to let his love, Criseyde, go. Yet some great scholars said, 'Nedely ther is noon, / But that fre chois is yeven us everychon' (There is no necessity; free choice is given to everyone). And other sly scholars said, 'If God seth al biforn— / Ne God may nat deceyved ben, parde— / Than moot it fallen, / . . . / That purveiance hath seyn before to be. / Wherfor I sey, that from eterne if he / Hath wist byforn oure thought ek as ourse dede, / We han no fre chois' (If God sees all before—indeed, God may not be deceived—then what providence has seen beforehand must happen. If God knew our thoughts and deeds from eternity, we have no free choice).[78]

51

"Others say, 'For nedfully byhoveth it nat to bee / That thilke thynges fallen in certayn / That ben purveyed; but nedly, as they sayn, / Byhoveth it that thynges whiche that falle, / That they in certayn ben purveyed alle' (It is not necessary that things happen because they have been foreseen; but it is necessary, as they [clerks] say, that all things that happen have been foreseen)," said Chaucer.[79]

"In other words," I said, "foreseen choices do not inform God of what he must will; rather, what God foresees is what he ordained to come to pass. But crucially, the necessity with which things happen is a mere conditional, or inferential, necessity. Troilus was distressed over whether somehow 'necessity' was planted in Criseyde's heart. Was he not free? Or was he born for her?"[80]

Commission: Ponder Troilus's dilemma: Is God's foreknowledge the certain cause of that necessity by which all things happen, or is the necessity of things to come the cause instead?[81]

Pss 37:4; 87:6; Prov 3:1–8; 31:1–31; Jer 1:5

27

Summè Perfectus et Summum Bonum

THIS LORD'S DAY, I met with Archbishop Thomas Bradwardine at Merton College, Oxford. I asked him about his view of God's will and freedom, about which he published in *De Causa Dei* (1334).

"Is it true that God is not so free as to ever decree that we dishonor our parents?" I asked.

"God is the 'highest perfection and highest good' (*summè perfectus et summum bonum*).[82] His essence—who he is—essentially restrains him from ever internally willing that he relinquish or forsake his own goodness and perfection. For instance, God cannot *not* beget God the Son.[83] As to this world, God's essence restrains him from ever decreeing, for instance, that we dishonor our parents. To love and honor our parents is something that goes deep into the very essence of who God is. The fact that 'God equally knows that which is non-being, which he brings into being, and that which he does not bring into being' speaks of his knowledge of all possibilities and his freedom to create.[84] Although the decree of God's will is most noble, nevertheless, it is not so free as to decree otherwise than that we honor our parents. To be created in God's image is at once to have inscribed upon our hearts that we honor our parents. Even so, the decree to honor our parents is dependent upon God's willing that it be so," he said.[85]

"So, the command to honor our parents goes beyond mere natural law. The command is very much tied to God's will and the seeds of this virtue he plants in our human hearts. Are there some things that are not necessary that God will them, but contingent?" I asked.

"Remember, when God wills what he wills for this world we live in, not only is it in accord with his very essence, but God himself is the end that moves his will; God acts 'for the sake of his holy name,' as Ezekiel wrote (Ezek 36:22). But when God acts to create and will a world into existence, he acts freely. Who would deny that God acts contingently when he freely gives us bread to eat, skills to use, languages to speak, life and light to illumine our path forward in this world?" he said.[86]

Commission: God himself is the end which moved him to create the world we live in. To give us all life and light, with the seeds of the virtue of love planted in our hearts by God our Creator.

Isa 43:1–28, 48:1–22; Ezek 36:22–32

28

Nunc Aeternitatis

THIS LORD'S DAY, I met the Westminster Assembly divine William Twisse (ca.1577–1646), who, together with Henry Saville, in 1618 edited and published Bradwardine's *De Causa Dei*. I asked him what was at stake in the doctrine of the immutability of God's decrees and human freedom.

"Defending God against the charge that he is the author of sin is what is at stake," he said. "Some theologians wish to lay maximum freedom and responsibility at your feet and mine in their scheme to protect God from the allegation of authoring sin. Their theory holds that God is present to us here in this world, and that things happen in a kind of 'eternal now' (*nunc aeternitatis*).[87] Hereby they wish to remove any sense of God's *pre*determining will."[88]

"So, what are the consequences of holding to this view? It seems to imply a concurrence of divine and human action. If so, would not God still be just as accountable for sinful acts as those who commit them?" I asked.

"You are familiar with Saint James's words: 'If the Lord wills, we will do this or that' (Jas 4:15 ESV). Well, these theologians wish to position the Lord's knowledge of our willing and his own willing in a commonly held 'eternal now.' I myself prefer what Duns Scotus said, which is closer to Saint James—namely, that if the Lord wills and thereby quickens our faculties, then he will know and see what will unfold, as you and I shall will to do whatever we do," he said.[89]

55

"What, then, is God's relation to our sinful actions, if any relation at all?" I asked.

"God's knowledge of our eating forbidden fruit, lying, cheating, coveting, or taking his name in vain, or whatever, is not such that he 'predetermines' or 'predefines' our *sinful* action. Nor does God learn afterwards of what we do and maneuver himself to escape responsibility. God's will precedes his visionary knowledge of what unfolds in this world. God's will establishes the time and place of future events and human action. God's knowledge of future, contingent events is ultimately based on the wise council of his will. But the moral character and thus responsibility of what you and I do belongs to us. Eating fruit is healthy—forbidden fruit, sinful.

Commission: Rejoice in the presence of God and ask him to prosper the work of your hands.

Deut 5:6–22; Pss 16:11; 90:1–17; Jas 1:13

29

The Neutral Proposition

THIS LORD'S DAY, I met Professor Gisbertus Voetius (1589–1676) at the University of Utrecht. I asked him about the eternal—beyond the bounds of time—acts of God's intellect and will.

"Have you ever heard of a neutral proposition? A proposition that God has in his mind about something or someone or some event in some possible world, which is not yet true and which may never be true? By 'true,' I mean that God has not yet decided whether he shall pass that particular being, or person, or state of affairs, or event, from a state of possibility into a state of futurity," he said.

"But in your scheme of things, it seems as if God's knowledge of himself changes?" I said.

"Not at all. Let me explain. God is pure Being. There is no shadow of change in his being. The question is, did God have to create everything he knows that he could create? No. So there is a difference between God's knowledge of all possible people, places, and things on the one hand, and God's knowledge of all real people, places, and things that are part of the world that God chose to create. Now I want you to imagine three moments in God's thought. But these are not real, time-bound moments. These three *moments* are for our way of thinking about God's interior thought life and what he knew was possible to create—creatable people, places, and things—and what God did in fact create to be part of this world in which we live. First, God exists and he knows himself and that he exists. As God said to Moses, 'I AM WHO I AM' (Exod 3:14). Second, God is related to people, places, and things outside himself, without any change to himself. Third, God is freely related to the people, places, and things that he passes, by his will, out of the state of possibility into futurity."[90]

"What is the benefit of thinking about God's thought life in this way?" I asked.

"God is free to will or not, or refrain from willing in his relation to what are otherwise neutral propositions concerning these people, places, and things. There is no necessary relation to them."[91]

Commission: God is free to will or not to will things into being. But he is not omnivolent. He does not will all that he possibly can will. Yet, God unfailingly accomplishes the best, the wisest, and the fittest choice for *his* world and *his* people.

Exod 3:14; Isa 40:13, 14; Matt 3:9; 26:53

30

Instantia Rationis

I RETURNED TO HARVARD College to meet again with Reverend Charles Morton. I asked him about the English textbook he had made for students which combined his teaching with doctrinal points abstracted from Leiden professor Adriaan Heereboord's *Pneumatica* text. I was very keen on exploring their teaching on the "three moments" that Professor Voetius had introduced to me last Lord's Day.[92]

"Even though God is pure Act and Being and is a living Spirit, in an accommodation to our way of thinking about God, there are three *moments*, or *instants* (*momenta naturae seu instantia rationis*), in the thought life of God, as it were, as regards God's act of decreeing whatever comes to be,"[93] said Reverend Morton. "To be sure, the decrees of God are eternal. Nevertheless, I remind our students that God's free act of determination of what he shall decree to pass into existence belongs to his internal, intra-Trinitarian life. In this sense the decrees are eternal—that is, beyond our conception of time and successive moments of time, of which there are none in God's intellect. On the other hand, whatever comes to fruition in the course of our lives clearly belongs to factual reality. Most of us are busy in our thoughts with God's relation to factual reality."

"Indeed. So, in a second *instant*, God has in mind a terminus, or end point, for the fruition of his decree. God's relation to the terminus is a transcendent relation (*relatio transcendentalis*).[94] But when does the act of God's decree relate directly to you and me in this world?" I asked.

"Remember, in the second instant, contrary to what we normally say of God, 'This relation to a terminus is something else in God besides God himself.'[95] Now, in the third instant, God's actual relation to people, places, and things comes into view. This instant differs from the interior, immanent, intra-Trinitarian activity and life of the first and second instants. God's decree now comes to fruition in our time-bound reality, our world, your life, and mine.

Commission: Apart from any utilitarian focus on yourself, ponder the intra-Trinitarian life of our God. God's love and glory move him to display his glory to us.

Exod 33:17–23; John 1:18; Col 1:15–17; 1 Tim 6:15–16

31

The Residue of the Spirit

I REMAINED AT HARVARD College to meet with Samuel Willard (1640–1707), the acting vice president (1701–7) and pastor of Third Church Boston.

"In your lectures on July 15 and August 12, 1690, to your church congregation on the Westminster Assembly's Shorter Catechism, you made what seemed to be an important distinction between an 'immanent' act of God and a 'transient' act of God. Could you explain?" I asked.[96]

"Yes. I was expositing the seventh and eighth questions of the Westminster Catechism. The questions are 'What are the decrees of God?' and 'How does God execute His decrees?' 'Since God works *in time*, we presuppose that he purposed to do so *before time*.'[97] God never was without this decree, and the word *immanent* appertains to the decree. 'In God we conceive some acts to be immanent, some to be transient.'[98] Crucially, the term 'immanent acts' of God speaks of the intra-Trinitarian acts that do not immediately affect you or me. On the other hand, the 'efficiency' of God's acts is *transient*, which means that the act 'falls upon an external subject' outside God himself, like upon you or me. 'This transient act leaves no change in God.' It only establishes a new relation between God and us. 'The only change is in the subject, which is passed out of possible being into future being,'" he said.[99]

"That brings me to my question about the meaning of 'the Residue of the Spirit,'" I said.[100]

"Very simply, God is able to do far more than he does. God has not gone to 'the utmost of his ability, but there was the residue of the Spirit with Him.' That means that there was, as it were, a 'partition between the possible beings, which never shall actually be, and those future things that shall in time have existence.' Possible beings 'wholly depend upon his will.'[101] The decree is the hinge upon which the door between the realm of possible beings and the realm of actual future beings turns. My friend, 'there is a vast company of possible beings in the knowledge of God; the decree appoints which of them shall be; which shall pass from possibility to futurition.'"[102]

Commission: Ponder God's infinite love, knowledge, and power, and that nothing but God's decree separates us from all those possible beings who never would be.

Gen 45:5–8; Job 23:14; Pss 119:89; 135:6; Mal 2:15 (KJV); Matt 10:29

32

A Double Conversion

I REMAINED IN BOSTON in order to learn more from Pastor Samuel Willard. I asked him to relate the efficiency of God's acts upon our faculties to our role in conversion.

He said, "'Recall that God's will is infinite and the first cause of things. Nothing but His will moved or inclined God's will.' Not our will but his will moved first. Furthermore, God's first act 'lays no forcible necessity on the creature, only certainty.'"[103]

"If God awakens my soul in the first act, does not my second act necessarily follow?" I asked.

"Remember that as part of the decree of his will, 'God has purposed that free agents shall act freely; as to the event, Christ's bones could not be broken, and yet there was no necessity cogent laid on the soldiers.'[104] I believe the Catechism teaches a 'passive' and 'active' conversion, or 'two-step conversion.'[105] You have learned about the logically structured 'order of nature.' In that order, God first moves upon our soul's powers, preparing the way for the second act so that you and I can 'exert the new principle infused' in the second step.[106] But you and I remain *passive* in the first step. Since God is acting at the physical level of our reality, there is no compulsion or coercion ascribable to God's first act. God is 'enabling us to comply with his invitation.'[107] Then, necessarily (an implicative necessity in consequence of the first free act), the second act follows upon the first. Now God goes to work in us as the 'author and finisher of our faith' (Heb 12:2). The Word and Spirit actively engage us. The 'formality' of the second act truly belongs to you and me."[108]

"The prophet Jeremiah and John the Baptist would be good examples of this 'double conversion,' as you call it," I said. "Both were called before birth; both believed in time."[109]

"Indeed. John, born with priestly blood from both parents, freely fulfilled his crucial role of identifying the perfect Lamb of God, Jesus the Messiah, to be offered up in Jerusalem," he said.

Commission: God's grace and power are at work in you, renewing your soul's powers, making evil a bitter thing to you and Jesus sweet, and revealing the mystery of the double conversion. "How few there be that are effectually called, and how vain the pretence of the most to a title to salvation."[110]

Job 23:13; Ezek 36:26; Matt 11:25; 20:16; Eph 4:22, 24; Phil 2:12, 13; Jas 1:18

33

Can the Justified Be Condemned?

BEFORE LEAVING BOSTON, I wanted to ask Pastor Willard about something he had said in his August 30, 1698 lecture about the possibility of being justified by God.[111]

"You said in that lecture to your church that 'a justified person can never again come under the law as guilty, in a compound sense. In a divided sense he may.'[112] I have heard about the divided sense from Bishop Bramhall, but I was curious about your application of the distinction in your teaching about justification. Could you explain the divided sense to me as applied in this context?" I asked.

"Certainly. I wished to instill 'an awe for the mystery of God's favor' in my people. To be sure, 'justification is immutable.' God shall not 'repeal' or 'repent' of the act. That is why I said that it is not possible that a justified person ever again be guilty under the law. However, I added the caveat that the proposition is true in the compound sense—that is, when read as a whole, without any commas. The compound reading applies the logic of non-contradiction. A person cannot both be guilty and justified at the same time. You cannot apply the predicate *guilty* to *justified*. You see the contradiction. But when you divide the reading of the proposition, it reads, 'A justified person, *may* come under the law as guilty.' I said 'may' in the sense that it is possible," he said. "At the *moment* in eternity of being declared justified, it is *possible* that the justified be condemned."[113]

"But why make the distinction in the first place?" I asked.

"To instill awe for the doctrine of justification and to challenge the deterministic thinking of many. I said, 'If God should leave him to himself, and take away his Spirit from him, he would fall out of grace.' But since the justified are secure 'under the new covenant, and the sure promises of it,' God cannot abandon the justified.[114] Similarly, Duns Scotus gave a lecture and asked, 'Can an elect be condemned?' He also taught that the proposition is false in the compound sense, but true in the divided sense."[115]

Commission: Be mindful of the ground upon which you persuade yourself that your sins are pardoned and God's just requirements met and satisfied. Rest in God's covenant love.

Jer 31:34; Isa 43:25; Acts 5:31; Rom 6:14; 8:2; 11:29

34

The Virgin Mystery

THIS LORD'S DAY, I visited the Benedictine monk Peter Damian (1007–72) to discuss his letter to Abbot Desiderius of the monastery of Monte Cassino about divine omnipotence.

"You wrote that while at table with the abbot, someone read a passage from Saint Jerome (ca. 347–419), who said, 'While God can do all things, he cannot cause a virgin to be restored after she has fallen.'[116] Jerome agreed that a virgin can of course be restored spiritually, and be freed from guilt. But you were not satisfied with the answer, since it implies that God is impotent. But in what sense can God restore someone's virginity once it is lost?" I asked.

"If God does not will to do something, does it mean that he cannot do it? I say no. God is not omnivolent, but he is omnipotent. Are there not many things you, a mortal, can do but do not? I wager there are. I ask you: 'What could hinder God from restoring a virgin after she has fallen?' I have already ruled out inability," he said.[117]

"Perhaps some people would think it an injustice to reverse someone's physical circumstance. And that therefore God would never do such an invasive, intrusive thing," I said.

"As to the merits of the case, recall Saint Paul, who promised the Corinthians in marriage to one husband, Christ, as 'a chaste virgin' (2 Cor 11:2). But the looming question is 'How can God bring it about that something that has happened will not have happened?'[118] Although I dislike using propositional logic when talking about God's omnipotence, nevertheless, for your sake, remember that 'God's ability [*posse*] to do all things is coeternal to God.' He is ever-present to the 'past, present, and future.'[119] Relative to God's 'unalterable eternity,' he '*can* so cause it to happen that Rome would not have been founded.' But relative to us, time passes, things change. Thus we say God could have [*potuit*] done so. Remember this: 'God's present never turns into the past. His today does not change into tomorrow.'[120] Since 'the potency to do all things is coeternal to God, then it follows that God could have caused things that have happened not to have happened,' such as in the case of one's lost virginity," he said.[121]

Commission: God is ever-present to you. He is never impotent. He is forever the great "I am."

Exod 3:14; Mal 2:6; John 8:58; 2 Cor 11:2; Jas 1:17; Rev 4:11

35

Can the Past Be Contingent?

THIS LORD'S DAY, I met Samuel Andrew (1656–1738), rector *pro tem* (1707–19) of Yale College in New Haven. He presided over the 1718 Yale bachelor commencement exercises, and one of the Latin theses listed on the broadside sheet intrigued me. Logic thesis 20 read: "A proposition about the past [*de praeterito*], can be contingent."[122]

What I had learned from other rectors about how to read a proposition with a comma in the divided sense taught me not to be too quick to apply the predicate, "contingent," to "the past," in the compound sense, lest I accept a contradiction. "How then can a proposition about the past be contingent?" I asked.

"Consider someone who was blind yesterday, but sees today," he said. "Would you not agree that the proposition about the past blindness was contingent, since now he sees? That is, 'He who was blind, can now see'? This is an obvious answer to your question. But suppose we translate *de praeterito* as 'from the past,' not 'about the past,'" he said.

"Then the thesis would read, 'A proposition about the past, can be contingent,'" I said. "But does that not imply that the past can be changed—that the past could be otherwise than it was?"

"Precisely. He who was blind yesterday, could possibly see yesterday. From our vantage point today, if he who was blind yesterday could have, at the same instant, not been blind, then today, possibly, he sees. The Latin *potest esse* in thesis 20, when read in the divided sense with the comma, highlights the possibility of a change in the status of the proposition," he said.

"Your student, Daniel Newell, copied a definition of contingency in a notebook," I said. "He wrote, 'Contingency is the essential disposition according to which reality can be otherwise than it is. The course of reality could have run otherwise in the divided sense, with respect to the attendant circumstances.'"[123]

"Indeed. The reality of this world, as far as God is concerned, can be otherwise than it is. Contingency can point to change over time, or to change at the same instant of time," he said.

Commission: Life is not one fixed, upward evolutionary progression. God's providence governs life, and at any moment he can answer prayer and alter the course of your life.

1 Sam 14:41; Job 23:13–14; Prov 16:33; Rom 9:13–26

36

The Euthyphro Mystery

THIS LORD'S DAY, I met Professor Voetius at Utrecht University to discuss the ancient dialogue of Euthyphro and Socrates at the entrance to the law courts in Athens.

"Now think of this," said Socrates. "Is what is holy holy because the gods approve it, or do they approve it because it is holy?"[124] After explaining that the noble cause precedes its effect, Socrates said, "We are agreed that the holy is loved because it is holy, and is not holy because it is loved. Isn't it so?" "Yes," answered Euthyphro.[125]

"In terms of my quest to exonerate the one true God from the charge that he is the author of sin," I said, "I am beginning to understand that God's commandments are not good because he decrees them so to be, but he commands them precisely because they are good and in line with his essential nature. Otherwise, hypothetically, some may wish to grant great freedom to God such that whatever God approves could be holy and good, even, for instance, the dishonoring of our parents or the literal offering up of our firstborn children for sacrifice. Isn't there a danger that, on the one hand, we grant too great a freedom to God, and on the other, that we limit God's freedom?" I asked.

"You are quite right to express this concern," said Professor Voetius. "There is no rule outside God himself that could govern his thoughts and precepts. We can trust God's character and honestly assert that something is good simply because God wills it so to be. God is subject to no one. He is no man's debtor. He is under obligation to none—that is, outside himself. On the other hand, God will not and cannot violate his own sense of justice."[126]

"Indeed. But certainly God has intra-Trinitarian obligations, would you not agree?"

"Yes. God loves the eternal Logos, his Son," he said. "When God makes covenant promises to his elect people, he will by all means keep his promises. Now, God is not above the law, but God may well will to test his subjects, such as he did with Abraham or Job."

Commission: The Euthyphro mystery requires another Lord's Day to ponder God's double will and how the precepts of God's will are never in conflict with the good pleasure of his will.

Gen 18:16–33; Ps 19:7–11; Rom 3:4–6

37

God's Double Will 1

THE EUTHYPHRO MYSTERY DISCUSSED last Lord's Day raised more questions concerning God's will as I continued my quest to understand why God is not the author of sin. I decided to spend the next four Lord's Days with Jonathan Edwards in his home in Stockbridge. I asked whether he was addressing this topic in his treatise *Freedom of the Will*.

"Indeed," he said. "I have a section in the treatise where I ask, 'Is God the author of sin?'"[127]

"Could you give me a preview and explain to me God's double will?" I asked.

"Yes. There is God's 'secret' will and there is God's 'revealed' will. The first corresponds to what I sometimes call God's 'disposing will,' what the schoolmen called *voluntas beneplaciti*. I sometimes call the second God's 'preceptive will,' what the schoolmen called *voluntas signi*.[128]

"Why do you sometimes call God's secret will his *disposing will*?" I asked.

"God is 'the all-wise disposer of all events,' even designer of all circumstances, is he not?[129] No doubt you have heard the maxim 'Man proposes, God disposes.' I am not afraid to affirm 'that if a wise and good man knew with absolute certainty, it would be best, all things considered, that there should be such a thing as moral evil in the world, it would not be contrary to his wisdom and goodness, for him to choose that it be so.'¹³⁰ For instance, to which of the two wills belongs Abraham's offering up of Isaac and the crucifixion of Christ, do you think?" he asked.

"To the first, God's *secret* or *disposing* will," I said. "But if so, even though the testing of Abraham and the crucifixion of Christ were part of God's wise plan, how do you resolve the apparent contradiction of these events with God's revealed will in the Ten Commandments?"

"Indeed, it is the first will, but contrary to what you think, God has good and desirable consequences in mind. Here is a key to understanding God's secret will: 'God may hate a thing as it is in itself,' such as crucifixion, yet it 'may be his will it should come to pass,'" he said.¹³¹

Commission: Though mortals will sin *as* sin, God never does.¹³² In the final issue, God's way is glorious. Mortals perpetrate horrific acts and store up wrath for themselves. Do not confuse the riches of God's kindness, forbearance, and patience with a future final judgment.

Deut 29:29; Jer 27:4–6; Rom 2:3–5; Acts 2:23; 3:12–21; Rev 17:17

38

God's Double Will 2

I WAS STILL UNEASY about the distinction between God's secret and revealed wills. This Lord's Day, I asked Rev. Edwards to explain the second of the two and how he resolved the apparent conflict of the one with the other.

"While at Yale, I learned from William Ames the old verse 'God instructs, forbids, permits, counsels, and fulfills.'[133] This is God's second will, the precepts that he has revealed in the Bible," he said. "Indeed, God's precepts forbid murder, yet God orders the crucifixion of his Son. But suppose God has 'opposite exercises of heart, respecting different objects' at the same time. God's 'will of choice' has the glorious good of the crucifixion before him. And God's 'will of refusal' has the evil of the 'malignant murderers' before him.[134] Is there a contradiction? No, there is no contradiction between God's secret will choosing the good and his revealed will refusing evil. But suppose God has it in his mind both to choose and to refuse the same object at the same time, 'to love both good and evil at the same time'—that would pose a contradiction, would it not?" he said.[135] "Likewise, if the distinction between God's two wills collapses the one into the other, then we will have difficulty absolving God from evil, won't we?"

"Indeed," I replied. "You said last Lord's Day that God hates evil for what it is, yet may will it to come to pass for a greater end. Now I understand the distinction a little better."

"Who will venture to say that there is no possible place in any divine design for evil?" he said. "'An infinitely wise Being, who always chooses what is best, must choose that there should be such a thing' as evil in the world. 'Such a choice is not an evil, but a wise and holy choice.'[136] Next Lord's Day, we shall continue our discussion of how it is God's good pleasure so to order and dispose *to permit* that 'evil should come to pass, for the sake of the contrary good.'"[137]

Commission: Ponder how God's will to permit such things does not mean that God does not "hate evil, as evil." Nor that God "may not reasonably forbid evil as evil, and punish it as such."[138]

Deut 2:30; Ps 105:16–25; Jer 51:20–23; Lam 3:37–38; Luke 22:21–22

39

The Mystery of God's Permissive Will

THIS LORD'S DAY, THE Reverend Jonathan Edwards explained to me the mystery of God's permissive will, the distinction between God permitting evil and God willing to permit evil.

"What is at stake in the Reformed theory of permission," said the Reverend Edwards, "is whether it absolves God from being the author of sin, and whether God positively decrees reprobation, as he does election.[139] There is, indeed, a distinction to be made between the mere divine permission of human action, on the one hand, and the divine production and authorship of the action itself, on the other. I prefer to discuss divine permission along the lines of God's positive will. To choose is to act electively. Concerning electing someone to salvation, God's willing *that not* Judas differs from the weaker position that God merely allows Judas to go his own way. Rather, God wills *not* to will to prevent Judas from going his own way. God is the 'permitter' and 'not a hinderer of sin.' Even with respect to evil, when God 'wills the disposal of such an event,' it is with a 'perfectly holy will.'[140] Thus, God's will of disposal is a positive act of will," he said.

"Your opponents say that your teaching on the necessity of God's decree of the will absolves people like Judas from any wrongdoing, and denies to others acts of virtue," I said.

"Indeed, they bring up the Stoic philosophers who said that 'In things necessary, the deficient cause must be reduced to the efficient."[141] In other words, they trace human vice and lapses of will back to God, who, they think, could have rescued the person in trouble or given assistance so that they not fail. But their position would make 'God the proper author of the unrestrained wickedness' of the devils themselves. I say that the only cause standing behind election and perseverance is God's secret, inscrutable will of good pleasure (*voluntas beneplaciti*)."[142]

Commission: As to the efficient cause of evil, as Edwards asks, "When the sun sets, is it the producer of darkness? No."[143] Ponder God's secret, sovereign will of good pleasure and freedom in election, such as of Mary, the mother of Jesus the Messiah; Salmon, the father of Boaz by Rahab; Ruth; and many more like them. And you and your generations of faith.

Isa 53:10–12; Matt 1:1–17; 26:36–56

40

The Mystery of the Messiah's Impeccability

BEFORE LEAVING THE REVEREND Jonathan Edwards in Stockbridge, I asked him, "How can God identify with our pain, grief, and trouble if, as you say, there are 'maxims of plain truth' that 'God is a perfectly happy Being, in the most absolute and highest sense possible'? That therefore, 'God is free from every thing that is contrary to happiness,' and that, strictly speaking, 'there is no such thing as any pain, grief or trouble in God'?"[144]

"I say this because no reasonable person can accept that God's infinite happiness be 'diminished' in any way, which is what would happen if he were to suffer what is infinitely 'disagreeable to him.' Can you imagine God enduring infinite pain and grief for every sin committed—enduring 'truly infinitely great crosses and vexations'? If so, God would be 'infinitely the most miserable of all beings.'[145] But there is the suffering Messiah," he said.

"Did not the Messiah genuinely identify with our pain, grief, and trouble, and his perfect holiness deserve his Father's praise?" I asked. "Yet, you have said that 'it was impossible, that the Messiah should fail of persevering in integrity and holiness.'[146] But 'surely he has borne our griefs'?"

"Even though God is 'infinitely happy' and 'above all capacity of receiving any benefit' from human beings, 'still he is worthy of our supreme benevolence for his virtue,'" he replied.[147] "Likewise, 'the Logos, who was with the Father, before the world, and who made the world, thus engaged in covenant to do the will of the Father in the human nature.'[148] This was a sure foundation. If it were at all shaky and liable to fail, then the Old Testament saints died without a Surety, and without a solid promise. Furthermore, Jesus the Messiah's own predictions of rising from the grave victoriously would have made him 'guilty of presumption.'[149] Some argue that Jesus, in order to genuinely merit virtue and praise, had to be truly free to do otherwise than fulfill the covenant that he made with the Father. But I say that the stronger the desire and will of Jesus the Messiah was to please the Father, and the further he was from indifference to obedience, the freer he was."[150]

Commission: Ponder Edwards's maxim "The stronger the inclination, and so the further from indifference, the more virtuous the heart, and so much the more praiseworthy the act" of Jesus the Messiah for us.[151]

Pss 40: 7–8; 116:12; Isa 42:1–4; 50:5–9; John 10:17–18, 15:10; Heb 4:15; 6:17–20

41

The Mystery of Evil

THIS LORD'S DAY, I visited with G. W. Leibniz in Hanover to discuss a select thesis in *Causa Dei,* published in 1710, the fourth appendix to his famous *Theodicy.* I asked him to explain to me how the following thesis helps absolve God from the charge that he is the author of evil:

> It is necessary that evil be possible, but contingent that evil be actual.[152]

"Indeed, it may sound strange to hear that the possibility of evil happening in this world is not accidental, but necessary. You have no doubt already learned along your journey that God has an infinite knowledge of all possible states of affairs, as we call them, and that this includes evil as a possible result of failed human action. But, as you recall, there is a distinction between what God knows as merely possible on the one hand, and what God knows and sees by virtue of the decree of his will on the other," he said.

"I learned the distinction from Peter van Mastricht and others—that it is the decree of God's will, as the hinge, that actualizes some, not all, of the possibilities, passing them into a state of futurition.[153] But how do I avoid the conclusion that God himself, with a possible object of evil before his mind, willed and thus produced that evil and its attendant circumstances?" I asked.

"Indeed. It is the 'Epicureans and Manicheans who attack us most violently on this very point.' Both virtue and vice belong to human behavior. Since no one is perfect, even good behavior is tainted with some selfish motive. Everyone has an angle, as they say. Our limitations, imperfections, and privations were all part of who we were even before we actually were—that is, while yet in a state of pure possibility. God saw Adam sinning while he was yet in that state.[154] I call that state the 'sphere of eternal truths or ideas that present themselves to the mind of God.'"[155]

"I see. If we had no imperfections or limitations, we would be like God," I said.

"Indeed. 'The very foundation of evil is necessary, but the origin of evil contingent,'" he said.[156]

Commission: Take comfort in the knowledge that God is not taken by surprise by evil in this world. "The LORD has made everything for its purpose, even the wicked for the day of trouble" (Prov 16:4).

Gen 50:20; Isa 6:1–13; 44:7; Ps 39:7–13; Prov 16:4; Eph 1:5,11

42

God's Best of All Possible Worlds

THIS LORD'S DAY, I remained in Hanover with the esteemed G. W. Leibniz, since I was intrigued by his correspondence with Caroline, Princess of Wales, and Rector Samuel Clarke, a Newtonian.

"In your first letter to Caroline," I said, "you wrote, 'Natural religion itself, seems to decay in England very much, and natural philosophy determines questions of liberty and fate.'"[157]

"Indeed, it seems that Newton's God has to tinker with the universe he created every once in a while. But I believe God made 'a beautiful pre-established order. . . . But when God works miracles, he does not do it in order to supply the wants of nature, but those of grace.'"[158]

"How do you respond to Rector Clarke, who holds that very often the 'sufficient reason' why things are the way they are, and not otherwise, is 'the mere will of God?'" I asked. "And that your preestablished order makes 'God no governor at all, but a mere necessary agent'?"[159]

"God has a 'supreme reason' that moves him 'to choose, among many series of things or worlds possible.' In fact, you and I make choices with God's concurrence. God's decree and movement upon our souls in no way 'changes' our choices, but only 'actualizes' our 'free natures, which he saw in his ideas,'" he said.[160]

"But if God chooses what is best, is he not constrained to do so, and thus not free?" I asked.

"Not at all," he said. "When God 'chooses what is best, he is not the less free upon that account: on the contrary, it is the most perfect liberty, not to be hindered from acting in the best manner.' When God chooses according to 'the most apparent good and the most strongly inclining good, he imitates therein the liberty of a truly wise being, in proportion to his disposition. Without this, the choice would be a blind chance.' Crucially, 'God's motive inclines without necessitating.' When God chooses the best among possibilities, 'what he does not choose, and is inferior in perfection, is nevertheless possible. But if what he chooses, was absolutely necessary; any other way would be impossible.'[161] Remember, the 'principle of what is best' is the sufficient reason why something that is contingent exists, and the motive that moves God."[162]

Commission: Ponder the idea that God's best of all possible worlds is just that—God's. His to conserve and preserve. In no way were all other possibilities outside of God's power.

Gen 1:31; 2:1–3; Ps 24:1, 2; 2 Pet 3:10–13

43

The Mystery of God's Supposed Middle Knowledge

THIS LORD'S DAY, I met with the Reverend John Leverett, who presided over the Harvard 1717 commencement exercises for the master's students. There was a *Quaestio* in Latin on the broadside sheet that caught my attention. Question 4 posed the following question: "Whether there is a certain third and middle knowledge in God, besides the knowledge of simple understanding and the knowledge of vision? This was denied by the respondent Nehemiah Hobart."[163]

I asked the Reverend Leverett, "What is at stake and what does one hope to gain by introducing a third kind of knowledge in God?"

"The Jesuit Luis de Molina (1535-1600) introduced the theory of middle knowledge (*scientia media*).[164] Molina positioned middle knowledge prior to God's will—prior in a logically ordered but nontemporal sense—but after God's knowledge of simple understanding. This gives God knowledge of future contingent states of affairs—that is, of people's actions, places, things, events, etc.—prior to God willing to pass these things out of a state of possibility into a state of futurity. God thus takes into account and reacts to future contingent human decisions. The Jesuits hoped to gain a genuine freedom of the human will. Here at Harvard, the Reverend Charles Morton saw a number of problems with middle knowledge. First, 'it is as if God barely foreknows future things.' Second, 'it impeaches God's wisdom.' Third, 'God sees now reasons.' Fourth, 'God is impotent to accomplish what he would do.' Fifth, 'it makes God as man, and man as God.'"[165]

"Why did the student respondent deny middle knowledge?" I asked.

"The student learned that propositions that appear before God's mind are either in a state of possibility or a state of futurity. The choice is binary. God does not gain knowledge of what you and I are doing in time before he himself has decreed it in eternity. The student rightly feared that middle knowledge conditioned God's knowledge and decree of the will," he said.

Commission: Ponder the origin of the lie that would make you and your kin masters of the universe and your wills independent of God in order to give you so-called freedom of will. Join the resistance, unmask the counterfeiter, and thank God every day for his sovereignty.

Matt 11:20–24; Acts 17:22–31; Eph 3:20

44

The Mystery of *Creabilis*, *Creandus*, and *Creatus*

THIS LORD'S DAY, I met again with Utrecht University professor Peter van Mastricht. I asked him to explain the distinctions between being creatable (*creabilis*), to be created (*creandus*), and being created (*creatus*), and why they matter. For it seemed to me that we were but a proposition in the decrees in the mind of God: whether he would elect us to be a member of the spouse of Christ—namely, the church—or not.[166]

"Although it is true that God created the world and all that unfolds in time in one pure act of the will, it is instructive for us to abstract the different nontemporal 'moments' of election and creation. If you think about it, in eternity past, people were proposed to God's mind (1) as 'creatable' and 'fallible' (*creabilis et labilis*), (2) as those 'to be created and to be fallen' (*creandus et lapsurus*), (3) as 'created and fallen' (*creatus et lapsus*), and (4) as 'rejected or reprobated' (*rejectus seu reprobus*). If I were to abstract different 'acts or moments' (*actus seu momenta*) of election, what do you think the first would be?" he asked.[167]

"I think that first and foremost, God would want to display his glory and mercy. Then, he finds objects suitable for his mercy. So at that moment, we would be considered as creatable and fallible," I said. "I suppose that God's decree that certain people would indeed be created follows."

"Precisely. God decrees to move people—you and me, for instance—from a state of being 'creatable' to a state of 'to be created,' and as such, to become objects of God's mercy. God's love then directs you and me to the 'highest and supernatural good' (*summum et supranaturale bonum*). God prepares and arranges the means of leading you and me to final salvation. He redeems you and me in the Messiah Jesus and applies his work to our hearts," he said.[168]

Commission: The language of *creabilis, creandus,* and *creatus* accentuates God's purposes in election and creation above whatever benefits you and I may receive in them. God wanted to display his glory, justice, and mercy, and it is a wonder that he found people like you and me to be suitable objects of his decree of mercy and love.

John 17:5–26; Eph 1:4–7; 1 Pet 1:1–5

45

The Law of Truth

IN 1642, RECTOR HENRY Dunster presided over the Harvard College commencement exercises. Logic thesis 12 read: "The precepts of the arts must be predicated of all, per se, and universally commensurate."[169] He told me that from these three rules, or laws, of Aristotle about necessary premises, professors like Peter Ramus (1515–72), William Ames, and Franco Burgersdijk extracted and taught three laws: (1) The law of truth (*lex veritatis*), (2) The law of justice (*lex justitiae*), and (3) The law of wisdom (*lex sapientiae*)."[170] This Lord's Day, I asked him to explain to me the first of these three laws and why they matter.

"Universally necessary premises are true in every instance of the subject," he said. "If I ask you, 'Are all human beings always just in their actions?' you would probably say, 'No, not always.' Likewise, 'Do living things grow?' It is likely that you would answer, 'Normally, but not always.' For each example, one can think of an exception. The answer is contingent upon the circumstances. So what would you say is true of all human beings in every instance?" he asked.

"All human beings are capable of laughter and language, and are mind gifted," I said.

"Precisely. Reasonable people would assent to the truth of what you just said about humans. To say that you are a human being is at the same time to say that you are an animal, a multicellular living organism that moves under your own volition. Thus, a human being is an animal. But not vice versa," he said.

"Why is it important to establish necessary premises in the first place?" I asked.

"These first principles establish immutable laws that in turn give infallibility to all instruction in the liberal arts. Consequently, you and I assent to the law of truth. And crucially, the stability of language about transcendent truths depends on these necessary premises," he said.

Commission: Propositions signify and affirm that something is true in reality. Remember, what is true in time was first true in God's mind in eternity. Every Lord's Day that we repeat the Lord's words "Take, eat; this is my body" and "Drink from the cup, all of you; for this is my blood of the covenant" (Matt 26:26-28), his words signify, affirm, and communicate the transcendental law of truth.

Matt 26:26-29; John 1:17; 17:17

46

The Law of Justice

This Lord's Day, Rector Dunster explained to me the meaning and significance of the second degree of necessary premises, which he and others call 'the law of justice.'

"The law of justice, as Ramus and Ames called it, says that the subject and predicate co-inhere in a kind of essential nexus.[171] The predicates are essential and necessary, per se. Let me explain. If I ask you, 'Are ravens black?' What would you answer?" he asked.

"Normally, yes. The predicate 'black' seems essential to the proposition about ravens," I said.

"Indeed. But let's be careful about what we say. A raven is not blackness, neither is blackness a raven. Black is just an adjective, an accidental predicate. But in the proposition 'A raven is black,' the subject and predicate form a nexus. Nevertheless, substance differs from accident, just as blackness differs from black, just as truth itself differs from something true, just as life differs from living," he said.

"I understand," I said. "For instance, necessarily, God is not merely true and good; he *is* truth and goodness. What examples did Aristotle give of essential, or per se, predication?" I asked.

"Aristotle's classic examples of essential predicates were 'Line belongs to triangle, point to line. For the very being or substance of triangle and line is composed of these elements. Odd and even belong to number.'[172] From this principle, Ramus and Ames abstracted the law of justice."

"But why does Ames call Aristotle's axiom 'the law of justice'?" I asked.

"The truest justice has to do with the principle of homogeneity. Ramus and Ames applied Aristotle's axiomatic law of justice 'to sift out of one liberal art any propositions that belonged to another.'[173] For instance, interdisciplinary theories of planetary motion imply that, for instance, Copernicus the mathematician and astronomer (1473–1543) crossed boundaries and entered the domain of astrophysics. Likewise, Ames very much wanted to guard for theology what belonged to theology. He considered metaphysics a usurper in this regard," he said.[174]

Commission: Does not your mind give assent to the law of justice, the principle of homogeneity, the principle of kindred spirits? These laws are first found in the truest, most just, and wisest God.

Gen 6:19–20; Pss 19:1–14; 89:14; Prov 1:1–7, 21:3

47

The Law of Wisdom

THIS LORD'S DAY, RECTOR Dunster explained to me the meaning and significance of the law of wisdom.

"The law of wisdom builds on the former two laws and is applied to define the limits and boundaries of the liberal arts program in the schools. In other words, wisdom measures the universality of all three laws. Let me show you how to apply the law of wisdom. In universally commensurate premises, there is a principle of reciprocity that comes into play. For example, 'Every human being, but only a human being, is capable of laughter.' This is known universally to be true, in any random case of the subject. Furthermore, Burgersdijk noted a reduplicative locution, which is: 'A human being, as a human being, is capable of laughter.'[175] Tell me," he said, "which statement is more necessary: 'A human being is an animal' or 'A human being is capable of laughter.'"

"Concerning the first, I suppose that a human being cannot *not* be an animal. But an animal *can* not be a human being. And for the second, a human being cannot *not* be capable of laughter. And that which is capable of laughter cannot *not* be a man. Thus, when wisdom applies the principle of reciprocity, the second proposition is reciprocal and universal, and thus has a stronger degree of necessity," I said.

"Precisely. The third law of predication is stronger than the second law, which in turn is stronger than the first law. The second law includes the first and the third includes the second, but the reverse order does not hold. So, every second-degree per se predication includes a first-degree predication. 'And every third-degree, universally commensurate predication includes a second-degree per se predication, but not vice versa,'" he said.[176]

Commission: Ponder now the three laws: the law of truth, the law of justice, and the law of wisdom. How does one complement and build upon the other in your life?

Prov 8:11–31; 9:9–10

48

The Square of Opposition

I REMAINED AT HARVARD and, on the Lord's Day, I asked the Reverend Morton to explain to me the meaning of the square of opposition and what it had to do with my quest to understand the liberty of the will, both God's and ours.

"Take out a sheet of paper and draw a square," he said. "Mark the top-left corner with the term 'willing' (*velle*). Mark the top-right corner with the term 'nilling' (*nolle*). Then mark the bottom-left corner with the term 'not nilling' (*non nolle*). And mark the bottom-right corner with 'not willing' (*non velle*). Think of the top-right corner, 'nolle,' in terms of willing the *absence* of something—for instance, the absence of love. And think of the bottom-right corner, 'non velle,' in terms of *negation*—for instance, not willing to love. Now draw a line from the top-left to the top-right corner. The schoolmen called this line the freedom of 'contrariety or the specification of act (willing and nilling). This is a liberty whereby a power is so indetermined as that it can will or nill—which are contrary species of action—any object proposed, whether it be good or evil; and the schoolmen say rightly that the will is not free in this sense.'"[177]

"I suppose the schoolmen argued that one needs to distinguish between 'good and evil, both real and apparent?'" I said, "since it is 'not the reality but the appearance that moves the will. A real good, appearing evil, may be nilled.'"[178]

"Precisely. Now I want you to draw a line from the top-left to the bottom-right corner. And from the top-right to the bottom-left corner. The schoolmen called these two lines the freedom 'of contradiction or as to the exercise of the act (willing or not willing good, nilling or not nilling evil). It is a liberty whereby a power is so indetermined, so that it can act or suspend its act, so say they. But I doubt it is true.'[179]

> This is how I teach my students to remember the square: "{Of contrariety is willing nilling} or {Of specifying acts is willing nilling}{Of contradiction is willing not willing} or {Of exercise is willing not willing}"[180]

Commission: God has uniquely gifted you with freedom of the will. As humans, you and I do not will evil *as* evil. But you and I must exercise discernment to distinguish apparent good from evil.
Josh 24:15–28; Matt 26:41; Mark 1:40–41; John 8:29; 21:22

49

The Square of Opposition Revisited

I REMAINED AT HARVARD in order to continue my talk with the Reverend Morton about the square of opposition. I had many questions yet to ask.

"Last Lord's Day, you told me that certain schoolmen—by which you meant the Jesuits, I believe—'place the liberty of the will, namely, in indifference to opposites privitive, acting or not acting.'[181] But does this apply to God?" I asked.

"No. God is pure act. So we cannot apply the term 'privitive' to God. But the terms 'willing' (*velle*) and 'willing that not' (*nolle*) do apply to God," he said.

"What is your understanding of the Reformed view of human liberty of the will?" I asked.

"First, it is important to recognize that we enjoy 'a liberty from compulsion and necessity.' Let me explain. Human beings share something in common with animals—namely, a natural internal inclination to do what we do. But we differ from brutes. 'A hungry horse seeing oats within his reach cannot forbear to eat,' but you and I can. To your question, 'Reformed philosophy places the liberty of the will not in indifference to opposites (willing or not willing, nilling or not nilling), but in a rational spontaneity, that is the will uninforced, following the practical understanding. It is impossible the will should not incline to a good proposed by the understanding, as not only good in itself, but at present good for us,' he said.[182]

"Let me be clear. I only deny the opponents' understanding of freedom of specification and exercise, since they place so much weight on indifference to good and evil. Reformed philosophy holds that moral agents like you and me incline to the good, as good, in and of itself. In sum, you and I act deliberately, rationally, and of our own accord."

"Before we finish today, where did the idea of the square of opposition come from?" I asked.

"It's origins are in antiquity.[183] When you see the four letters *AEIO* in a logic textbook, like Arnauld and Nicole's *Port Royal Logic*, 1683 edition, the letters represent the four corners of the square of opposition, beginning from top left to right, then bottom left to right," he said.[184]

Commission: Ponder the difference between what appears good to us at the moment and what we are willing to forbear for the greater, long-term good, for the truth, for Messiah's kingdom.

Luke 22:39–46; Rom 7:7–25

50

The Essence of Free Choice

STAYING AT HARVARD AFFORDED me the opportunity this Lord's Day to meet with Increase Mather (1639–1723), president of Harvard. I asked him to explain to me the matter I had encountered last Lord's Day concerning whether indifference be the essence of freedom of the will, or rational spontaneity, as the Reverend Morton had told me, or something else.

"In 1694, I presided over a Harvard master's *Quaestio* on 'whether indifference be essential to freedom of choice.' The respondent was Timothy Edwards, and he denied this was the case," he said.[185] "In order to answer your question, there is an important distinction to be made in faculty psychology between 'free choice' (*liberum arbitrium*) and the will (*voluntas*). The Latin idiom underlying the translation 'free choice' includes the notion of an arbiter, a judge. The judgment of our free choice freely seeks one way or another to obtain happiness, one way or another to find a spouse. Our judgment is marked by indifference in the sense that we weigh and consider our options, the means to obtain the desired end. Our judgment and intellect also inform our faculty powers of willing (*velle*), nilling (*nolle*), and not willing (*non velle*)," he said.

"I have learned that the will (*voluntas*) itself has to do with freedom of specification (e.g., to love or to will not to love) and freedom of exercise (e.g., to love God or forbear to love God). Thus, whereas the act of our will eliciting a choice is decisive in willing the ultimate end desired, our judgment is *indifferent* and not necessitated or compelled one way over another. But then why did Timothy Edwards deny that indifference is the essence of free choice (*liberum arbitrium*)?" I asked.[186]

"The essence of God's freedom is not in indifference. In a fallen state, sinners are not indifferent concerning good and evil. Born-again believers experience a daily renewal of their judgment and will concerning what is good. In heaven, the saints are not indifferent to the beatific vision. In sum, the essence of freedom is to be found in rational willingness," he said.[187]

Commission: God is not indifferent in his love toward his beloved Son, Jesus the Messiah, nor to us in him. God loves us freely, heals our disloyalty, and turns his anger away when we return.

Hos 14:4; John 3:16; 2 Cor 4:16

51

The Self-Determining Power of the Will

I STILL HAD MANY questions in my mind about the power of the will in the matter of free choice, since it appeared that there were different, well-nuanced opinions even among the Reformed theologians themselves. This Lord's Day, I sat down with Elisha Williams, who was Jonathan Edwards's tutor from 1716 to 1719 and the fourth Rector of Yale, serving from 1726 to 1739.

"In 1735, I presided over the Yale commencement exercises. Metaphysics theses 6 and 7 read, 'Divine foreknowledge does not deny human liberty' and 'The will is the power of the mind determining itself.'[188] As you know, our students are required to read William Ames's *Marrow of Theology*. He wrote, 'Man of his own accord freely fell from God' and 'Although the freedom of the will essential to man's nature remains, this bondage destroys the freedom which belongs to the perfection of human nature and includes the power to perform acts spiritually good and acceptable—or at least the bondage leaves that freedom remote and dead.'"[189]

"How do you reconcile his theses that appear to teach that freedom of the will remains intact after the fall on the one hand, but the power to will the good is lost on the other?" I asked.

"The Reformed tradition distinguished between *formal* freedom and *material* freedom.[190] Formally, the freedom of the will remains intact, since you and I remain created after the *imago Dei*.

Materially, the freedom to will, achieve, and perform the good is lost after the fall. God, however, is slowly restoring the reach of material freedom of the will. Do you recall Professor Gisbertus Voetius? He taught that the essence of free choice is that the will is master of its own act. Now, if the greatest goal in your life is to glorify God, do you think there is but one determined means to achieve that end?" he asked.[191]

"No. Not only do I have many possible means in mind, but God has an infinite number of possible means at his disposal. I suppose my mind and will are indifferent in regards to choosing the means to achieve the end, with alternate possibilities available at the instant I decide," I said.

Commission: God's mercies are new every morning. Ask him daily to renew and sanctify the purposes of your heart, mind, strength, and soul to glorify the name of the Lord forever.

Lam 3:21–33; Mark 12:28–34; Rom 12:1–2; 16:25–27

52

God Is No Minister of Fate

This Lord's Day, I met with Jonathan Edwards at Stockbridge. I asked him about his thoughts on the so-called chain of being and of fate, since he spoke against the claim that his "Calvinist"—that is, Reformed—faith, amounted to nothing more than fate. From all I had learned visiting with him in the past, and with many different rectors and professors, I knew that this was not at all true.

"I made notes about this very topic in my *Controversies Notebook*," he said. "I asked, 'If there were a chain hung down out of the heavens to earth, what holds up the chain?'[192] The answer I often get from my opponents is that 'one link is held up by the next,' ad infinitum."

"But that does not answer the question, does it? I presume that God holds up the chain," I said.

"The point I want to make is that these links in the chain, as it were, and the whole chain, does do not just hang together by chance. The question is, Who or what determines the sequence of each link in the chain? One must arrive at a first Being, God himself. My opponents, the Arminians, want the sequence to depend on what God sees will happen '*in time*,' before it exists in God's eternal decrees.[193] They say, 'God foreknows things are future antecedent to God's decree, and independent of it.' If what they say is true, then 'God has no power by his decree to make anything future or not; he has no choice in the case.'[194] I say, 'nothing can be the cause of the existence' of any event without God's decree of the will. They say that God's foresight of people's choices is the cause behind what God decrees. I say that 'the divine decree must be the ground of the futurition of the events, and also the ground of God's foreknowledge.'"[195]

"Then God himself is the first cause who holds up the chain." I said.

"Precisely. But God is no 'minister of fate,' as some charge, in determining the sequence of events that will unfold in time. For God, who is 'the first Being, self-existent, independent, of perfect and absolute simplicity and immutability, and the first cause of all things, always chooses what is wisest and best,' according to his 'universal determining providence,'" he said.[196]

Commission: Pray for God to enlarge your heart and soul to embrace his mysteriously chosen portion and cup for your life. As it is in heaven, so shall his will be done for you on earth.

Exod 21:12–13; Pss 16:5–11; 33:1–22; Lam 3:37–38; 1 Cor 1:26—3; Matt 6:10.

Chapter Endnotes

Week 1

1. Junius, *True Theology*, 107 (§7); *Opuscula Theologica Selecta*, 41, 51.
2. Trelcatius, *Briefe Institution*, 1-2. Original Latin source: *Scholastica et Methodica*, 9. Trelcatius's *Scholastica et Methodica* is listed in the Yale University Library Catalog at https://orbis.library.yale.edu/vwebv/holdingsInfo?bibId=1312985. For more on the making of the early Yale college library, see Mooney, *Eighteenth-Century Catalogues*.
3. Ames, *Marrow of Theology*, 95 (§15).
4. Trelcatius, *Briefe Institution*, 2; Ames, *Marrow*, 96 (§25). Cf. Muller, *Prolegomena to Theology*, 232.

Week 2

5. Ames, *Technometry*, 100.
6. Trelcatius, *Briefe Institution*, 2.
7. Ames, *Technometry*, 100-101, 112, 146-47.
8. Junius, *True Theology*, 113 (§8). Original Latin Source: *Opuscula Theologica Selecta*, 41, 53.

Week 3

9. Vos, "Logos Title," 59.
10. Vos, "Logos Title," 65-66.
11. Kuyper, *Near unto God*, 304 (§56).

Week 4

12. "Clarke's Answer to Bulkeley's Third Letter," in Clarke, *Demonstration*, 130. See Fisk, "Moral Necessity," 173.
13. Duns Scotus, *Divine Love*, 64-77. "Because God's will always has the right direction *by itself*, his knowledge is merely presenting and not guiding,

CHAPTER ENDNOTES

which is the opposite of the way human knowledge functions. God's theoretical knowledge precedes his will and necessarily determines it. God does not have any practical knowledge which is a guide preceding his acting." His knowledge of "prescribed acts which precedes them, he knows as neutral, without any truth-value" (Duns Scotus, *Contingency and Freedom*, 107 [§§44]).

Week 5

14. Fisk, "Divine Knowledge," 154–55. Translations mine.

15. Ames, *Marrow of Theology*, 96 (§25). Translation mine, given the need to translate the Latin idiom *posse* as "can," not "may," and the need to correct the suggestion that it is "through" God's most perfect knowledge that he brings things about. Rather, in §25 it is left unspecified, but in §27 Ames makes it clear that what God knows by his knowledge of vision he knows *ex decreto*. Original: "Scientia simplicis intelligentiae est omnium possibilium, id est, rerum universarum et singularum, quae fieri possunt, perfectissima in Deo scientia" (Ames, *Theologiae Medullae*, 31 [§25]) Citations are from Eusden's English translation of Ames's *Medullae*, unless otherwise indicated.

16. Trelcatius, *Briefe Institution*, 70.

Week 6

17. For an introduction to Charles Morton, see Kennedy, *Aristotelian and Cartesian Logic*, 62–93; see also Burden, *Biographical Dictionary*, 381–94.

18. Williams, *Ethicks and Pneumaticks*, seq. 64. I have supplied a few words to make the text more readable. Morton abstracted these texts from Heereboord's *Pneumatica* and translated them into English. The *Pneumatica* was appended to Heereboord, *Meletemata Philosophica*.

19. Williams, *Ethicks and Pneumaticks*, seq. 64. See http://nrs.harvard.edu/urn-3:HUL.ARCH:10919374?n=2.

20. Williams, *Ethicks and Pneumaticks*, seq. 64.

21. "Omnivolent" appears in the English translation of Ames's *Marrow of Theology*, 99. Although the term itself means that God is "all-willing," Ames denied that God is omnivolent. It is a translation of the Latin *omnivolens*.

On Jonathan Edwards's and Johann Friedrich Stapfer's thoughts on this same subject, see Fisk, "Tension." For the thoughts of Samuel Willard (1640–1707), vice president of Harvard (1701–7), on this same topic, see Fisk, "Que Sera, Sera."

Week 7

22. Heereboord, *Meletemata Philosophica*, 176. For more on Heereboord's notion of "God's negative indifference," see Fisk, *Edwards's Turn*, 149.

23. On negative indifference, see Heereboord, *Meletemata Philosophica*, 176.

CHAPTER ENDNOTES

Week 8

24. Goodwin, *Exposition of Ephesians*, 105. Thomas Goodwin: BA 1616–17 and MA 1620 (St Catherine's Hall, Cambridge); BD 1630 and DD 1653 (Oxford); president of Magdalen College, Oxford (1650–60). For a biography and information about Goodwin's role as an "Independent" and member of the Westminster Assembly, see Joel R. Beeke's introduction in Goodwin, *Exposition of Ephesians*, [1–23]. See also Jones, *Why Heaven Kissed Earth*. Cf. Michael J. McClymond, "Hearing the Symphony: A Critique of Some Critics of Sang Lee's and Amy Pauw's Accounts of Jonathan Edwards' View of God," in Schweitzer, *Jonathan Edwards*, 91–92n63.
25. Goodwin, *Exposition of Ephesians*, 105.
26. Goodwin, *Exposition of Ephesians*, 105.

Week 9

27. Goodwin, *Exposition of Ephesians*, 120–21; Edwards, *"Miscellanies,"* 177–81.
28. Goodwin, *Exposition of Ephesians*, 121; Edwards, *"Miscellanies,"* 178–79.
29. Goodwin, *Exposition of Ephesians*, 121.
30. Edwards, *"Miscellanies,"* 178–80.

Week 10

31. Goodwin, *Exposition of Ephesians*, 121.
32. Goodwin, *Exposition of Ephesians*, 121.
33. Goodwin, *Exposition of Ephesians*, 121.
34. Goodwin, *Exposition of Ephesians*, 121.
35. Goodwin, *Exposition of Ephesians*, 112.

Week 11

36. Van Mastricht, *Theoretico-Practica Theologia*, 395–96 (Q. 2). Translation mine. Original: "An in providentia, talis detur *influxus* Dei, quo *physice* praedeterminet *omnes* omnino causas ad agendum?" See Fisk, "Petrus van Mastricht," 113–15.
37. Van Mastricht, *Theoretico-Practica Theologia*, 398 (Q. 5). Translation mine. Original: "An influx ille praedeterminans, Deum faciat auctorem peccati?"
38. Van Mastricht, *Theoretico-Practica Theologia*, 399 (Q. 7). Translation mine. Original: "An circa peccatum providentia divina, non occupetur, nisi oitiosa permissione, seu mera *anergeia*?"

Week 12

39. Charnock, *Existence and Attributes*, 1:340–45.
40. Charnock, *Existence and Attributes*, 1:342.

Chapter Endnotes

Week 13

41. Schaff, *Evangelical Protestant Creeds*, 3:486–87.
42. Schaff, *Evangelical Protestant Creeds*, 3:606.
43. Charnock, *Existence and Attributes*, 1:342.

Week 14

44. Charnock, *Existence and Attributes*, 1:343.
45. Charnock, *Existence and Attributes*, 1:344.

Week 15

46. Charnock, *Existence and Attributes*, 1:446.
47. Charnock, *Existence and Attributes*, 1:446.

Week 16

48. Andreas J. Beck, "The Will as Master of Its Own Act: A Disputation Rediscovered of Gisbertus Voetius (1589–1676) on Freedom of Will," in Asselt, *Reformed Thought*, 145.
49. Bramhall, *Works*, 719. See Fisk, *Edwards's Turn*, 285. For a modern introduction to the Bramhall-Hobbes debate, as well as selections from their treatises, see Chappell, *Hobbes and Bramhall*, xi, 85.
50. Bramhall, *Works*, 715; Chappell, *Hobbes and Bramhall*, 61. See Fisk, *Edwards's Turn*, 282.

Week 17

51. On the "fallacy of division," see Arnauld and Nicole, *Logic*, 199.
52. On the "order of nature" (*signum rationis*), see Fisk, *Edwards's Turn*, 255, 297–300; and Edwards, *Freedom of the Will*, 177–79, 190–94.
53. The ecumenical enterprise using these scholastic distinctions needs acknowledgement, whether Anglican, Presbyterian, Dutch Reformed, Dominican, or Franciscan. On the medieval Franciscan use of this exact term of art, "priority of nature," by Peter John Olivi (1248–98), Marenbon writes, "Nor is it enough to say that, at instant t^1 the will has the power to choose or not to choose to φ, at the next instant, t^2. Olivi wants to insist (*Commentary on Sentences* II, q.57 ad 10) that at instant t^2 itself the will can choose or not choose to φ at t^2, and that although there is only one instant of time involved, there is a priority of nature between its choice of will at t^2 and its acting in accord with it at t^2. Olivi argues that if, in some way, the will loses its freedom to φ or not to φ at t^2 when passing from t^1 to t^2, then it is not in fact free with regard to how it acts at t^2. The synchronous non-Aristotelian conception of modalities that underlies this account and is strongly suggestive of the modal innovations for which Scotus would be celebrated (Study L) is extended also to God's willing,

Chapter Endnotes

although Olivi is unhappy to describe divine volition as being 'contingent'; rather, it is 'free'" (Marenbon, *Medieval Philosophy*, 280; see also 288–93). On "synchronic contingency" and the divided sense, see Vos, *Scotus, Contingency, and Freedom*, 26–28, 108–17, 123–27, 187.

54. Bramhall, *Works*, 719; Chappell, *Hobbes and Bramhall*, 44. See Fisk, *Edwards's Turn*, 282.

Week 18

55. Bramhall, *Works*, 718. "5th Axiom: All the reality or perfection in something exists formally or eminently in its first and total cause" (Arnauld and Nicole, *Logic*, 250).

56. Burgersdijk, *Institutionum Logicarum*, 69. Translation mine. Original: "XXI. Causa Principalis vel aequalis est effecto, vel nobilior." On this same principle, see Ames, "Theses logica," in *Philosophemata*, 163: "Omnis causa natura prior est suo effecto, et etiam prior dignitate, quatenus nempe effectum ab ipsa dependet [Every cause is structurally prior to its effect, and even prior in dignity, to the extent that naturally the effect depends upon it]" (Ames, *Philosophemata*, 163 [§27], translation mine).

57. Duns Scotus, *Contingency and Freedom*, 96, 102, 104.

58. "Whether the necessity of a decree denies the liberty and contingency of a creature? Respondent Peter Thachery denied it." ("1674, original," in *Quaestiones*, box 9, folder 16). "Whether the root of contingency in second causes is God's will itself? Respondent Samuel Wiswall affirmed it" ("1704, original," in *Quaestiones*, box 9, folder 44). Translation mine.

Week 19

59. Charnock, *Existence and Attributes*, 1:450. On whether it was in Peter's power to deny or not to deny Christ, see the disputation in the year 1465 in Louvain, Belgium (Peter De Rivo, "A Quodlibetal Question on Future Contingents," in Schoedinger, *Readings in Medieval Philosophy*, 254–59). For the underlying Latin, see Baudry, *La Querelle*, 70–78.

60. Charnock, *Existence and Attributes*, 1:446–47.

Week 20

61. On divine concurrence and "whether physical predetermination" (*An praedeterminatio Physica*) makes God the author of sin, see Rutherford, *Disputatio Scholastica*, 383–93.

62. For the classic example of the praise and blame of voluntary versus involuntary actions with regard to throwing goods overboard, see Aristotle, *Nicomachean Ethics*, in *Basic Works*, 964–65 (1109b30–1110a30).

CHAPTER ENDNOTES

Week 21

63. Rutherford, *Disputatio Scholastica*, 378. A representative of the other viewpoint to which Rutherford refers may be, for instance, the Jesuit cardinal Robert Bellarmine (1542–1621).
64. Rutherford, *Disputatio Scholastica*, 384.

Week 22

65. Rutherford, *Disputatio Scholastica*, 376–77.

Week 23

66. Stapfer, *Institutiones Theologicae*, 1:109–10; Rutherford, *Disputatio Scholastica*, 101–11.
67. Stapfer, *Institutiones Theologicae*, 1:109–10.
68. For Leibniz's description of Muslim fate, Stoic fate, and Christian fate, and the orgin of the term *fatum*, see Alexander, *Leibniz-Clarke Correspondence*, 58 ("Leibniz's Fifth Paper").

Week 24

69. John Dryden, "The Cock and the Fox," in Hammond and Hopkins, *Poems of John Dryden*, 353–54 (lines 509–16). On this question of Dryden and Chaucer, see Fisk, "Que Sera, Sera," 283–85.
70. John Dryden, "The Cock and the Fox," in Hammond and Hopkins, *Poems of John Dryden*, 353–54 (lines 523–24, 528–30, 533–35, 538–41).
71. John Dryden, "The Cock and the Fox," in Hammond and Hopkins, *Poems of John Dryden*, 353–54 (lines 542–45).

Week 25

72. Geoffrey Chaucer, "The Nun's Priest's Tale," in Benson, *Riverside Chaucer*, 258–59 (lines 3246–50).
73. Geoffrey Chaucer, "The Nun's Priest's Tale," in Morrison, *Portable Chaucer*, 200.
74. Geoffrey Chaucer, "The Nun's Priest's Tale," in Benson, *Riverside Chaucer*, 258 (lines 3240–42). Editor Henry Savile (1549–1622), warden of Merton College, cites lines 3234–51 of Chaucer's "The Nun's Priest's Tale" in his preface to the reprint of Thomas Bradwardine's *De Causa Dei*, iv.
75. Bradwardine uses and explains the term "necessite condicionel" in *De Causa Dei*, 715.
76. Geoffrey Chaucer, "The Nun's Priest's Tale," in Benson, *Riverside Chaucer*, 258–59 (lines 3234–50). For "inferential necessity," see Benson, *Riverside Chaucer*, 259n3250. The term "necessite condicionel" is from Chaucer's translation of Boethius's *The Consolation of Philosophy*: see "Boece," in

CHAPTER ENDNOTES

Riverside Chaucer, 468 (lines 178–83). For the editor's explanatory note, see 939–40n3245–60.

Week 26

77. Geoffrey Chaucer, "Troilus and Criseyde," in Benson, *Riverside Chaucer*, 551 (lines 980, 982, 1000).
78. Geoffrey Chaucer, "Troilus and Criseyde," in Benson, *Riverside Chaucer*, 550–51 (lines 961–62, 970–80).
79. Geoffrey Chaucer, "Troilus and Criseyde," in Benson, *Riverside Chaucer*, 551 (lines 1003–8).
80. See Geoffrey Chaucer, "Troilus and Criseyde," in Benson, *Riverside Chaucer*, 552 (lines 1082–95).
81. See Geoffrey Chaucer, "Troilus and Criseyde," in Morrison, *Portable Chaucer*, 496–97.

Week 27

82. Bradwardine, *De Causa Dei*, 1.
83. Bradwardine, *De Causa Dei*, 657.
84. Bradwardine, *De Causa Dei*, 229.
85. Bradwardine, *De Causa Dei*, 228–34. "Sed existentia conditionis, scilet quod ista creatura est, causetur et dependet a voluntate divina. [But the existence of the condition—namely, that this creature is, is caused by, and depends upon the divine will.]" (231, translation mine).
86. Bradwardine, *De Causa Dei*, 657.

Week 28

87. S.v. "*aeternitas*" in Muller, *Dictionary*, 18.
88. Twisse, *Dissertatio de Scientia Media*, 124, 349.
89. Twisse, *Dissertatio de Scientia Media*, 341.

Week 29

90. Beck, *Voetius*, 347–48.
91. Beck, *Voetius*, 357–58.

Week 30

92. Williams, *Ethicks and Pneumaticks*, seq. 71; Heereboord, *Pneumatica*, 78; Fisk, *Edwards's Turn*, 215–17.
93. Heereboord, *Pneumatica*, 78. On "instantia," s.v. "momentum" in Muller, *Dictionary*, 222.
94. Heereboord, *Pneumatica*, 78; Williams, *Ethicks and Pneumaticks*, seq. 71.

CHAPTER ENDNOTES

95. Heereboord, *Pneumatica*, 78; Williams, *Ethicks and Pneumaticks*, seq. 71. This quote is my own rephrasing of Heereboord, adapted from the text of Williams's English notebook.

Week 31

96. Willard, *Compleat Body*, 102, 105 (lectures 32–33). In reference to Willard's *Compleat Body of Divinity*, Holifield says, "After its posthumous publication in 1726, the *Compleat Body* became an authoritative text in American Reformed theology for the next half century" (Holifield, *Theology in America* 62).
97. Willard, *Compleat Body*, 101 (lecture 32).
98. Willard, *Compleat Body*, 102 (lecture 32).
99. Willard, *Compleat Body*, 105 (lecture 33).
100. Willard, *Compleat Body*, 101 (lecture 32). For more on Willard's notion of "the residue of the Spirit," see Fisk, "Que Sera, Sera," 293–94.
101. Willard, *Compleat Body*, 101 (lecture 32).
102. Willard, *Compleat Body* 102 (lecture 32).

Week 32

103. Willard, *Compleat Body*, 103 (lecture 32).
104. Willard, *Compleat Body*, 103 (lecture 32).
105. Willard, *Compleat Body*, 457, 819 (lectures 121, 226).
106. Willard, *Compleat Body*, 819 (lecture 226).
107. Willard, *Compleat Body*, 819 (lecture 226).
108. Willard, *Compleat Body*, 458 (lecture 121).
109. For more on the idea of double conversion and these two examples, see Fisk, "Que Sera, Sera," 292.
110. Willard, *Compleat Body*, 461 (lecture 121).

Week 33

111. Willard, *Compleat Body*, 465–67 (lecture 123).
112. Willard, *Compleat Body*, 466 (lecture 123).
113. Willard, *Compleat Body*, 466.
114. Willard, *Compleat Body*, 466.
115. Duns Scotus, *Divine Love*, 131–45.

Week 34

116. Peter Damian, "On Divine Omipotence," in Wippel and Wolter, *Medieval Philosophy*, 143; Marenbon, *Medieval Philosophy*, 116–18. "Damian was in fact concerned with the same temporal necessity which caused trouble in the statistical interpretation of modality. If is is true that what is, necessarily is,

Chapter Endnotes

when it is, then at whatever moment of time the actual state of affairs excludes all alternative states of affairs with respect to that time as impossibilities. Now Damian is not contented to say that these 'impossibilities' are Divine possibilities. Instead he maintains that God can make things with mutually exclusive properties, which is tantamount to denial of the law of Contradiction" (Knuuttila, *Great Chain of Being*, 201; see 200–203).

117. Peter Damian, "On Divine Omipotence," in Wippel and Wolter, *Medieval Philosophy*, 145.

118. Peter Damian, "On Divine Omipotence," in Wippel and Wolter, *Medieval Philosophy*, 147.

119. Peter Damian, "On Divine Omipotence," in Wippel and Wolter, *Medieval Philosophy*, 147.

120. Peter Damian, "On Divine Omipotence," in Wippel and Wolter, *Medieval Philosophy*, 148.

121. Peter Damian, "On Divine Omipotence," in Wippel and Wolter, *Medieval Philosophy*, 149.

Week 35

122. Saltonstall, *Commencement Broadside*. Translation mine. Original: "*Propositio de praeterito, potest esse contingens.*"

123. Newell, *Student Notebook*. Translation mine. Original: "Q. 24. Quid est contingentia? Reply: Contingentia est natura affectio secundum quam natura potest aliter se habere qua habet. Q. 25 Quibus respectibus natura dicitur se aliter habere quam habet? Reply: Natura potuit se aliter habere sensu divisos respectu circumstantiarum et adjunctorum separibilium."

Week 36

124. Plato, "Euthyphro," 178 (10a).

125. Plato, "Euthyphro," 179 (10e).

126. See Beck, *Voetius*, 366–69. Concerning God's will: "If it has any cause, something must precede it, to which it is, as it were, bound; this is unlawful to imagine.... Nevertheless, we fancy no lawless god who is a law unto himself. For, as Plato says, men who are troubled with lusts are in need of law; but the will of God is not only free of all fault but is the highest rule of perfection, and even the law of all laws" (Calvin, *Institutes*, 949–50 [3.23.2]). Cf. Burton, "Euthyphro Dilemma," 122–40.

Week 37

127. Edwards, *Freedom of the Will*, 397–412.

128. Edwards, *Freedom of the Will*, 407, 434.

129. Edwards, *Freedom of the Will*, 410.

130. Edwards, *Freedom of the Will*, 411.

Chapter Endnotes

131. Edwards, *Freedom of the Will*, 407.
132. Edwards, *Freedom of the Will*, 408–9.

Week 38

133. Ames, *Marrow of Theology*, 100 (§54).
134. Edwards, *Freedom of the Will*, 407.
135. Edwards, *Freedom of the Will*, 407.
136. Edwards, *Freedom of the Will*, 407–8.
137. Edwards, *Freedom of the Will*, 409.
138. Edwards, *Freedom of the Will*, 409.

Week 39

139. On the origins of willing to allow (*volens sinere*), see Lombard, *Sententiae*, 316 (I 46 ch. 3). For the English translation, see Lombard, *Mystery of the Trinity*, 250. For the Latin, see Lombard, *Sententiae*, 316 (I 46.3).
John Duns Scotus adapts the Lombardian notion of "willing to allow" and formulates a new theory of a second-order volition. For the second-order of volition, see Vos, *Theology*, 297–300; Duns Scotus, *Divine Love*, 188. Cf. Fisk, "Edwards's Conception of Election." S.v. "permission" and *"permissio efficax"* in Muller, *Dictionary*, 259.
140. Edwards, *Freedom of the Will*, 399.
141. *Freedom of the Will*, 397, 404. Translation mine. Original: "Causa deficiens, in rebus necessariis, ad causam per se efficientem reducenda est."
142. Edwards, "*Miscellanies*," 180.
143. Edwards, *Freedom of the Will*, 404.

Week 40

144. Edwards, *Freedom of the Will*, 409.
145. Edwards, *Freedom of the Will*, 409–10.
146. Edwards, *Freedom of the Will*, 286. Cf. Fisk, "Impeccability of Jesus Christ," 309–25.
147. Edwards, *Freedom of the Will*, 280.
148. Edwards, *Freedom of the Will*, 287.
149. Edwards, *Freedom of the Will*, 287–88.
150. The Latin idiom "freedom *ad utrumque*" (freedom to choose either of two things), which triggered such a negative reply by Edwards in his *Freedom of the Will*, was commonly used with careful nuance by both Reformed and Arminian theologians. The Latin term appears in Edwards, *Freedom of the Will*, 203, 204, 279, 289, 290, 455.
151. Edwards, *Freedom of the Will*, 320–21.

CHAPTER ENDNOTES

Week 41

152. Leibniz, *Opuscules Philosophiques Choisis*, 272–73 (§69). Translation mine.
153. See weeks 5 and 6 above. Leibniz says, "That which is not contingent passes from potency to act by virtue of the universal harmony, due to its agreement with the best sequence of things, of which it is a part" (Leibniz, *Opuscules Philosophiques Choisis*, 272–73 [§69], translation mine).
154. Leibniz, *Theodicy*, 346 (§369).
155. Leibniz, *Opuscules Philosophiques Choisis*, 272–73 (§§68–69).
156. Leibniz, *Opuscules Philosophiques Choisis*, 272–73 (§69).

Week 42

157. Alexander, *Leibniz-Clarke Correspondence*, 6, 11 ("Clarke's Dedication," "Leibniz's First Paper").
158. Alexander, *Leibniz-Clarke Correspondence*, 12 ("Leibniz's First Paper").
159. Alexander, *Leibniz-Clarke Correspondence*, 20–21, 30, 50 ("Clarke's Second Reply," "Clarke's Third Reply," "Clarke's Fourth Reply").
160. Alexander, *Leibniz-Clarke Correspondence*, 56 ("Leibniz's Fifth Paper").
161. Alexander, *Leibniz-Clarke Correspondence*, 56–57 ("Leibniz's Fifth Paper").
162. Alexander, *Leibniz-Clarke Correspondence*, 57 ("Leibniz's Fifth Paper").

Week 43

163. "1717, original," in *Quaestiones*, box 9, folder 56. Translation mine. For the Harvard 1717 *Quaestiones* broadside sheet, see https://iiif.lib.harvard.edu/manifests/view/drs:428670851$1i. S.v. "*scientia media*" in Muller, *Dictionary*, 326.
164. Molina, *On Divine Foreknowledge*, 13n20, 23, 46–62, 228–30.
165. Williams, *Ethicks and Pneumaticks*, seqs. 10 and 67. Cf. Ames, *Marrow of Theology*, 96 (§28). For Williams's student notebook, see http://nrs.harvard.edu/urn-3:HUL.ARCH:10919374?n=2 The idea that "God sees now reasons" implies that future contingents condition God's knowledge; the theory ascribes deliberations and ratiocination to God, which Morton and other Reformed theologians find unacceptable. On Morton and middle knowledge, see Fisk, *Edwards's Turn*, 201–4.

Week 44

166. Fisk, "Edwards's Conception of Election." S.v. "*supra lapsum*" in Muller, *Dictionary*, 348–49.
167. Van Mastricht, *Theoretico-Practica Theologia*, 293, 304. Francis Turretin posed the following question: "Whether the object of predestination was man creatable, or capable of falling; or whether as created and fallen? The

former we deny; the latter we affirm" (Turretin, *Topics*, 376 [Topic 4, Q. 9]). Cf. "The first objects of election may be *res creabiles, non tantum quae actu creatae sunt et existunt,*—things that are looked upon by him but as yet to be created, not only those that are supposed actually to exist" (Goodwin, *Exposition of Ephesians*, 82; see also 117). On this terminology, see Pollmann, *Historical Reception of Augustine*, 1186.

168. Van Mastricht, *Theoretico-Practica Theologia*, 293. See Barth, *Doctrine of God*, 132–33 for Karl Barth on this exact text and Van Mastricht's mediating distinction between *homo creabilis et labilis* as the object of God's purpose, and *homo creatus et lapsus* as the object of election.

Week 45

169. Morison, *Founding of Harvard College*, 439. Translation mine. Original: "Praecepta Artium debent esse κατὰ παντὸς, καθ' αὑτό, καθ ὅλου πρῶτον."

170. Ames, *Technometry*, 99–100, 107, 144–46, 163–65 (§§40, 42, 78–81); Burgersdijk, *Institutionum Logicarum*, 131. See Fisk, *Edwards's Turn*, 52–54; Aristotle, *Posterior Analytics*, in *Basic Works*, 115–16 (73a21–73b9). On Aristotle's necessary premises, see Kneale and Kneale, *Development of Logic*, 94–96.

Week 46

171. Burgersdijk, *Institutionem Logicarum*, 131. Jonathan Edwards learned this second degree of necessary predication—that is, the essential nexus between subject and predicate—and would write about it in *Freedom of the Will*, 152–54.

172. Aristotle, *Posterior Analytics*, in *Basic Works*, 116 (73a35–39).

173. Ames, *Technometry*, 163.

174. Ames, *Technometry*, 39.

Week 47

175. Burgersdijk, *Institutionem Logicarum*, 132. Translation mine. Original: "Homo, qua homo, est risibilis."

176. Burgersdijk, *Institutionem Logicarum*, 133. Translation mine. Original: "Hoc est, omnis enunciato per se, est etiam de omni; et omnis enunciato universaliter prima, est etiam per se: sed non vice versa." The following are Aristotle's examples of commensurate predication: "Point and straight belong to line essentially, for they belong to line as such. Triangle as such has two right angles, for it is essentially equal to two right angles" (Aristotle, *Posterior Analytics*, in *Basic Works*, 117 [73b26–30]).

CHAPTER ENDNOTES

Week 48

177. Williams, *Ethicks and Pneumaticks*, seqs. 8–9. To view the notebook online, see https://nrs.harvard.edu/urn-3:HUL.ARCH:10919374?n=2). See also Fisk, *Edwards's Turn*, 223–27.
178. Williams, *Ethicks and Pneumaticks*, seqs. 8–9. See Fisk, *Edwards's Turn*, 226.
179. Williams, *Ethicks and Pneumaticks*, seq. 8. See Fisk, *Edwards's Turn*, 225.
180. Williams, *Ethicks and Pneumaticks*, seq. 9. See Fisk, *Edwards's Turn*, 227.

Week 49

181. Williams, *Ethicks and Pneumaticks*, seq. 8. See Fisk, *Edwards's Turn*, 225.
182. Williams, *Ethicks and Pneumaticks*, seq. 9. See Fisk, *Edwards's Turn*, 227–29.
183. Kneale and Kneale, *Development of Logic*, 55–56, 86, 125–26, 210.
184. Authors of logic textbooks mapped opposite kinds of acts of the will onto a teaching tool commonly called a "square of opposition." Likewise, with respect to necessity and possibility, textbooks mapped opposing relations onto the square of opposition. See Watts, *Logick*, 158–59. For a recent English translation, see Arnauld and Nicole, *Logic*, 84–86, 143–56; cf. The "Doctrine of opposition scheme" in Wesley, *Compendium of Logic*, 9, 10. Cf. The "square of opposition" in Asselt, *Reformed Thought*, 34, 45. On John Wesley's use of "liberty of contradiction" and "liberty of contrariety," and Vos's conclusion that, at least from a systematic point of view, Wesley's use of this distinction places him in the Reformed tradition, see Vos, "John Wesley," 203–22. See also Fisk, *Edwards's Turn*, 191, 224–31, 310.

Week 50

185. "1694, original," in *Quaestiones*, box 9, folder 33. For the Harvard 1694 *Quaestiones* commencement broadside, see https://nrs.harvard.edu/urn-3:HUL.ARCH:30876656?n=1. "An indifferentia sit de essentia liberi arbitrii? Negat respondens Timotheus Edwards" (Morison, *Seventeenth Century*, 629). That both sides of this concept were disputed is evident in the Harvard 1691 bachelor's physics thesis 29: "Indifferentia est de essentia liberi arbitrii [Indifference is the essence of free choice]," presided over by tutors John Leverett and William Brattle ("1691, original," in *Theses*, box 1, folder 11, translation mine). For the Harvard 1691 theses commencement broadside, see https://nrs.harvard.edu/urn-3:HUL.ARCH:29087120?n=1. All translations mine. On the Harvard 1694 *Quaestio* on indifference, see Fisk, *Edwards's Turn*, 86–88, 120–31, 151–66.
186. Morison, *Seventeenth Century*, 629.

Chapter Endnotes

187. Asselt, *Reformed Thought*, 182–86. The Reformed theologian Francis Turretin (1623–87) argued in the *Tenth Locus* on *Free Choice* that he does not dispute that there is freedom of indifference in the first act, which is God's freedom of acting (or possibility of not acting) to move upon the soul to awaken it and enable it to respond to his love. Nor does he dispute that there is indifference in the divided sense, since he affirms the individual's faculty of *simultas potentiae*, the simultaneity of potency. But Turretin denies what he calls Jesuit, Socinian, and Remonstrant freedom of indifference in the composite sense, in which it is alleged that the individual can exercise *potentia simulatatis*, the potency of simultaneity. The problem with the latter is that contradictory objects of the will cannot be willed simultaneously. What is accepted by Turretin is that when you choose A, it is possible that you choose not-A. See Francis Turretin, *First through Tenth Topics*, in Asselt, *Reformed Thought*, 171–200 (Topic 10, Q. 1-1-3). For an older translation, see Turretin, *Topics*, 659–683. S.v. *"simultas potentiae"* in Muller, *Dictionary*, 336.

Week 51

188. Theses 6 ("Praescientia divina non tollit libertatem humanam") and 7 ("Voluntas est mentis sese determinandi potestas"), in Tallcott, *Yale College Commencement Broadside*. All translations mine. Aaron Burr and Joseph Bellamy were commencers that day, both taking their bachelor's degree.

Jonathan Edwards argued against freedom of will and for a freedom of perfection, in the sense that the stronger the previous bias and inclination to one choice, the freer the will is. He rejected the so-called self-determining power of the will, in both God and humans. He associated the concept with his opponents, the Arminians. See Edwards, *Freedom of the Will*, 278, 298, 323, 332, 360, 375, 391, 414, 421, 429, 433, 436, 445, 453–54, 463, 466, 470. Cf. Fisk, *Edwards's Turn*, 393–94, 407–8, 414–15.

189. Ames, *Marrow of Theology*, 114, 119 (§§11, 44).

190. See Dekker and Veldhuis, "Freedom and Sin," 155.

191. Andreas J. Beck, "The Will as Master of Its Own Act: A Disputation Rediscovered of Gisbertus Voetius (1589–1676) on Freedom of Will," in Asselt, *Reformed Thought*, 145–70.

Week 52

192. Edwards, *"Controversies" Notebook*; *Controversies Book C*. Access the original notebook online at Yale University Library: https://collections.library.yale.edu/catalog/10687815. On the great chain of being, see Lovejoy, *Great Chain of Being*, and an important critique of Lovejoy's thesis in Knuuttila, *Reforging the Great Chain*.

193. Edwards, *Controversies Book C*, 281.

194. Edwards, *Controversies Book C*, 279.

195. Edwards, *Controversies Book C*, 281.

Chapter Endnotes

196. Edwards, *Freedom of the Will*, 377. Edwards's interlocutor, whom he brought into his discussion, was Isaac Watts, who had previously written that those who taught that God determines things by an antecedent superior fitness of things make God to be a "mechanical medium of fate" and introduce "Hobbes's doctrine of fatality"—in short, making God a "minister of fate." For Edwards's reply to Watts, see Edwards, *Freedom of the Will*, 375–96. See also Fisk, *Edwards's Turn*, 397–99.

Bibliography

Alexander, H. G., ed. *The Leibniz-Clarke Correspondence Together with Extracts from Newton's* Principia *and* Opticks. Manchester, UK: Manchester University Press, 1998.
Ames, William. *The Marrow of Theology*. Based on 3rd Latin edition 1629. Translated and edited by John D. Eusden. Grand Rapids: Baker, 1997.
———. *Philosophemata*. Amsterdam: Joannem Janssonium, 1651.
———. *Technometry*. Translated and edited by Lee W. Gibbs. Philadelphia: University of Pennsylvania, 1979.
———. *Theologiae Medullae*. Edited by James S. Candlish. First published 1648. Reprint, London: James Nisbet & Co., 1874.
Anselme. *Monologion, Proslogion*. Translated by Michel Corbin. L'Œuvre d'Anselme de Cantorbéry 1. Paris: Éditions du Cerf, 2008.
———. *Pourquoi Dieu S'est Fait Homme: Texts Latin, Introduction, Bibliographie, Traduction et Notes*. Translated by René Roques. Sources Chrétiennes 91. Paris: Éditions du Cerf, 2005.
Aristotle. *The Basic Works of Aristotle*. Edited by Richard McKeon. New York: Random House, 1941.
Arnauld, Antoine, and Pierre Nicole. *Logic or the Art of Thinking, Containing, Besides Common Rules, Several New Observations Appropriate for Forming Judgment*. Translated and edited by Jill Vance Buroker. Cambridge Texts in the History of Philosophy. Cambridge: Cambridge University Press, 1996.
Asselt, Willem Jan van, et al., eds. *Reformed Thought on Freedom: The Concept of Free Choice in Early Modern Reformed Theology*. Texts and Studies in Reformation and Post-Reformation Thought. Grand Rapids: Baker Academic, 2010.
Barth, Karl. *The Doctrine of God*. Vol. 2, bk. 2 of *Church Dogmatics*. Edited by G. W. Bromiley and T. F. Torrance. Translated by J. W. Edwards et al. Edinburgh: T. & T. Clark, 1958.
Baudry, Léon, ed. *La Querelle des Futurs Contingents (Louvain 1465–1475)*. Études de Philosophie Médiévale 38. Paris: J. Vrin, 1950.

Bibliography

Beck, Andreas J. *Gisbertus Voetius (1589-1676): Sein Theologieverständnis und seine Gotteslehre*. Forschungen zur Kirchen- und Dogmengeschichte 92. Göttingen: Vandenhoeck & Ruprecht, 2007.

Benson, Larry D. *The Riverside Chaucer*. 3rd ed. Oxford: Oxford University Press, 2008.

Bradwardine, Thomas. *De Causa Dei Contra Pelagium et de Virtute Causarum Ad Suos Mertonenses Libri Tres*. Edited by Henry Savile. London: John Bill, 1618.

Bramhall, John. *The Works of the Most Reverend Father in God, John Bramhall D. D., Late Lord Bishop of Ardmagh, Primate and Metropolitan of All Ireland. Some of Which Never Before Printed. Collected into One Volume*. Vol. 3 of *The Castigations of Mr. Hobbes, His Last Animadversions in the Case Concerning Liberty and Universal Necessity*. Dublin: Benjamin Tooke, 1677.

Burden, Mark. *A Biographical Dictionary of Tutors at the Dissenters' Private Academies, 1660-1729*. London: Dr Williams's Centre for Dissenting Studies, 2013.

Burgersdijk, Franco. *Institutionum Logicarum, Libri Duo*. London: Roger Daniels, 1651.

Burton, Simon. "Samuel Rutherford's Euthyphro Dilemma: A Reformed Perspective on the Scholastic Natural Law Tradition." In *Reformed Orthodoxy in Scotland: Essays on Scottish Theology 1560-1775*, edited by Aaron Clay Denlinger, 122-40. London: Bloomsbury Academic, 2014.

Calvin, John. *Calvin: Institutes of the Christian Religion*. The Library of Christian Classics 20-21. Edited by John T. McNeill. Translated by Ford Lewis Battles. Philadelphia: Westminster, 1960.

Chappell, Vere, ed. *Hobbes and Bramhall on Liberty and Necessity*. Cambridge Texts in the History of Philosophy. Cambridge: Cambridge University Press, 1999.

Charnock, Stephen. *The Existence and Attributes of God*. First published 1853 by Robert Carter & Brothers. Reprint, Grand Rapids: Baker, 1996.

Clarke, Samuel. *A Demonstration of the Being and Attributes of God, and Other Writings*. Edited by Ezio Vailati. Cambridge Texts in the History of Philosophy. Cambridge: Cambridge University Press, 1998.

Cobban, Alan B. *The Medieval English Universities: Oxford and Cambridge to c. 1500*. London: Routledge, 2017.

Dekker, Eef, and Henri Veldhuis. "Freedom and Sin: Some Systematic Observations." *European Journal of Theology* 3 (1994) 153-61.

Duns Scotus, John. *Duns Scotus on Divine Love: Texts and Commentary on Goodness and Freedom, God and Humans*. Translated and edited by Antonie Vos Jaczn et al. Aldershot: Ashgate, 2003.

———. *John Duns Scotus: Contingency and Freedom, Lectura I 39*. Translated and edited by Antonie Vos Jaczn et al. The New Synthese Historical Library 42. Dordrecht: Kluwer Academic, 1994.

Bibliography

———. *A Treatise on God as First Principle: A Latin Text and English Translation of the de Primo Principio*. Translated and edited by Allan B. Wolter. Chicago: Franciscan Herald Press, 1966.

Edwards, Jonathan. *Controversies Book C. Notebook*. From Beinecke Rare Book and Manuscript Library, *Jonathan Edwards Collection, 1696–1972*. https://collections.library.yale.edu/catalog/10687815.

———. *"Controversies" Notebook*. Vol. 27 of Works of Jonathan Edwards Online. Jonathan Edwards Center, Yale University, 2008. http://edwards.yale.edu/research/browse.

———. *Freedom of the Will*. Vol. 1 of *Works of Jonathan Edwards*. Edited by Paul Ramsey. New Haven: Yale University Press, 1957.

———. *The "Miscellanies," 1153–1360*. Vol. 23 of *Works of Jonathan Edwards*. Edited by Douglas A. Sweeney. New Haven: Yale University Press, 2004.

Fisk, Philip John. "Divine Knowledge at Harvard and Yale: From William Ames to Jonathan Edwards." *Jonathan Edwards Studies* 4 (2014) 151–78.

———. "Jonathan Edwards and Alexander Gottlieb Baumgarten: Aesthetic Theology and the Art of Beautiful Thinking." In *Edwards, Germany, and Transatlantic Contexts*, edited by Rhys S. Bezzant, 111–31. New Directions in Jonathan Edwards Studies 8. Göttingen: Vandenhoeck & Ruprecht, 2021.

———. "Jonathan Edwards and Samuel Clarke on Moral Necessity: A Matter of Distinction, and Why It Matters." *Jonathan Edwards Studies* 10 (2020) 167–79.

———. "Jonathan Edwards's Conception of Election and Freedom of the Will." In *The T. & T. Clark Companion to Election*, edited by Edwin Chr. van Driel. Place: Bloomsbury, forthcoming.

———. "Jonathan Edwards's *Freedom of the Will* and His Defence of the Impeccability of Jesus Christ." *Scottish Journal of Theology* 60 (2007) 309–25.

———. *Jonathan Edwards's Turn from the Classic-Reformed Tradition of Freedom of the Will*. New Directions in Jonathan Edwards Studies 2. Göttingen: Vandenhoeck & Ruprecht, 2016.

———. "Petrus van Mastricht and Freedom of the Will." In *Petrus van Mastricht (1630–1706): Text, Context, and Interpretation*, edited by Adriaan C. Neele. Reformed Historical Theology 62. Göttingen: Vandenhoeck & Ruprecht, 2020.

———. "Que Sera, Sera. The Controversial 1702 Harvard Commencement *Quaestio* on Whether the Immutability of God's Decree Takes Away Human Freedom of the Will." In *Jonathan Edwards within the Enlightenment: Controversy, Experience, and Thought*, edited by John T. Lowe and Daniel N. Gullota, 283–98. New Directions in Jonathan Edwards Studies 7. Göttingen: Vandenhoeck & Ruprecht, 2020.

———. "The Tension Between Jonathan Edwards's 'Controversies' Notebook and Freedom of the Will on Whether Reality is Open and Contingent." In *The Global Edwards: Papers from the Jonathan Edwards Congress Held*

Bibliography

in Melbourne, August 2015, edited by Rhys S. Bezzant, 121–35. Australian College of Theology Monograph Series. Eugene, OR: Wipf & Stock, 2017.

Goodwin, Thomas. *Exposition of Ephesians*. Vol. 1 of Nichols Series of Standard Divines. First published 1861 by James Nichol (Edinburgh). Reprint, Lafayette, IN: Sovereign Grace, 2001.

Hamilton, Edith, and Huntington Cairns, eds. *The Collected Dialogues of Plato, Including the Letters*. Bollingen Series 71. Princeton: Princeton University Press, 1980.

Hammond, Paul, and David Hopkins, eds. *The Poems of John Dryden: Volume Five: 1697–1700*. Longman Annotated English Poets. London: Routledge, 2014.

Heereboord, Adriaan. *Meletemata Philosophica*. Amsterdam: Joannem Ravesteinium, 1665.

Holifield, E. Brooks. *Theology in America: Christian Thought from the Age of the Puritans to the Civil War*. New Haven: Yale University Press, 2003.

Jones, Mark. *Why Heaven Kissed Earth: The Christology of the Puritan Reformed Orthodox Theologian, Thomas Goodwin (1600–1680)*. Göttingen: Vandenhoeck & Ruprecht, 2010.

Junius, Franciscus. *Opuscula Theologica Selecta*. With a preface by Abraham Kuyper. Bibliotheca Reformata. Amsterdam: Muller & Kruyt, 1882.

———. *A Treatise on True Theology: With the Life of Franciscus Junius*. Translated by David C. Noe. Grand Rapids: Reformation Heritage, 2014.

Kennedy, Rick, ed. *Aristotelian and Cartesian Logic at Harvard: Charles Morton's A Logick System & William Brattle's Compendium of Logick*. Publications of the Colonial Society of Massachusetts 67. Boston: Colonial Society of Massachusetts, 1995.

Kneale, William, and Martha Kneale. *The Development of Logic*. Oxford: Clarendon, 2008.

Knuuttila, Simo, ed. *Reforging the Great Chain of Being: Studies of the History of Modal Theories*. Synthese Historical Library: Texts and Studies in the History of Logic and Philosophy 20. Dordrecht: D. Reidel Publishing Company, 2010.

Kuyper, Abraham. *To Be Near unto God*. Grand Rapids: Eerdmans-Sevensma, 1918.

Leibniz, Gottfried Wilhelm. *Gottfried Wilhelm Leibniz: Opuscules Philosophiques Choisis*. Translated and edited by Paul Schrecker. Bibliothèque des Textes Philosophiques. Paris: J. Vrin, 2001.

———. *Theodicy: Essays on the Goodness of God, the Freedom of Man, and the Origin of Evil*. Edited by Austin Farrer. Translated by E. M. Huggard. Rare Masterpieces of Philosophy and Science. New Haven: Yale University Press, 1952.

Lombard, Peter. *The Mystery of the Trinity*. Bk. 1 of *The Sentences*. Translated by Giulio Silano. Mediaeval Sources in Translation 42. Toronto, Canada: Pontifical Institute of Mediaeval Studies, 2007.

Bibliography

Lombard, Peter. *Sententiae in IV Libris Distinctae*. Spicilegium Bonaventurianum 4. Grottaferrata, Rome: Editiones Collegii S. Bonaventurae Ad Claras Aquas, 1971.

Lovejoy, Arthur O. *The Great Chain of Being: A Study of the History of an Idea*. Cambridge, MA: Harvard University Press, 1936.

Marenbon, John. *Medieval Philosophy: An Historical and Philosophical Introduction*. London: Routledge, 2009.

McKeon, Richard, ed. *The Basic Works of Aristotle*. New York: Random House, 1941.

Molina, Luis de. *On Divine Foreknowledge: Part IV of the Concordia*. Translated by Alfred J. Freddoso. Ithaca: Cornell University Press, 1988.

Mooney, James E., ed. *Eighteenth-Century Catalogues of the Yale College Library*. New Haven: Yale University Beinecke Library, 2001.

Morison, Samuel Eliot. *The Founding of Harvard College*. Cambridge: Harvard University Press, 1995.

———. *Harvard College in the Seventeenth Century*. Vol. 2. Cambridge: Harvard University Press, 1936.

Morrison, Theodore, trans. and ed. *The Portable Chaucer*. Rev. ed. New York: Penguin, 1977.

Muller, Richard A. *Dictionary of Latin and Greek Theological Terms: Drawn Principally from Protestant Scholastic Theology*. 2nd ed. Grand Rapids: Baker Academic, 2017.

———. *Divine Will and Human Choice: Freedom, Contingency, and Necessity in Early Modern Reformed Thought*. Grand Rapids: Baker Academic, 2017.

———. *Prolegomena to Theology*. Vol. 1 of *Post-Reformation Reformed Dogmatics*. 2nd ed. Grand Rapids: Baker Academic, 2003.

Newell, Daniel. *Student Notebook 1700–1731*. GEN MSS Vol 17. Beinecke Library, Yale University. https://hdl.handle.net/10079/bibid/3915074.

Novikoff, Alex J. *The Medieval Culture of Disputation: Pedagogy, Practice, and Performance*. Philadelphia: University of Pennsylvania Press, 2013

Plato. *Euthyphro*. In *The Collected Dialogues of Plato, Including the Letters*, edited by Edith Hamilton and Huntington Cairns. Bollingen Series 71. Princeton: Princeton University Press, 1961.

Pollmann, Karla, ed. *The Oxford Guide to the Historical Reception of Augustine*. Vol. 2. Edited by Willemien Otten. Oxford: Oxford University Press, 2013.

Quaestiones, 1653–1791. Broadsides. From Harvard University Archives, Commencement Theses, Quaestiones, and Orders of Exercises. https://id.lib.harvard.edu/ead/hua03010/catalog.

Rutherford, Samuel. *Disputatio Scholastica de Divina Providentia, Variis Praelectionibus, Quod Attinet ad Summa Rerum Capita, Tradita s. Theologiae Adolescentibus Candidatis in Inclytâ Academiâ Andreapolitanâ, in Quâ Adversus Iesuitas, Arminianos, Socinianos, de Dominio Dei, Actione Ipsius Operosâ Circa Peccatum, Concursu Primae Causae, Praedeterminatione & Contenditur & Decertatur*. Edinburgh: Haeredes Georgii Andersoni pro Roberto Brouno, 1649.

Bibliography

Saltonstall, G. *Yale College Commencement Broadside.* Early American Imprints, Series I: Evans 1639–1800. New London: Timothy Green, 1718.

Schaff, Philip, ed. *The Evangelical Protestant Creeds.* Vol. 3. *The Creeds of Christendom.* 6th ed. Grand Rapids: Baker, 1996.

Schoedinger, Andrew B. *Readings in Medieval Philosophy.* Oxford: Oxford University Press, 1996.

Schweitzer, Don, ed. *Jonathan Edwards as Contemporary: Essays in Honor of Sang Hyun Lee.* New York: Peter Lang, 2010.

Stapfer, Johann Friedrich. *Institutiones Theologicae Polemicae Universae, Ordine Scientifico Dispositae.* Vol. 1. Tiguri, Zürich: Heideggerum et socios, 1756–57.

Tallcott, Joseph. *Yale College Commencement Broadside.* Early American Imprints, Series I: Evans 1639–1800. New London: Timothy Green, 1735.

Theses, 1642–1818. Broadsides. From Harvard University Archives, *Commencement Theses, Quaestiones, and Orders of Exercises.* https://id.lib.harvard.edu/ead/hua03010/catalog.

Trelcatius, Lucas, Jr. *Scholastica et Methodica Locorum Communium.* Hanover: Guilielmum Antonium, 1610.

———. *A Briefe Institution of the Common Places of Sacred Divinitie. Wherein, the Truth of Every Place is Proved, and the Sophismes of Bellarmine Are Reproved.* Translated by John Gawen. London: Francis Burton, 1610.

Turretin, Francis. *First through Tenth Topics.* Vol. 1 of *Institutes of Elenctic Theology.* Edited by James T. Dennison Jr. Translated by George Musgrave Giger. Phillipsburg, NJ: P. & R., 1992.

Twisse, William. *Dissertatio de Scientia Media Tribus Libris Absoluta, Quorum Prior Gabrielem Penottum ad Partes Vocat in Suo Libertatis Humanae Propugnaculo: & ad Quindecem Capita Posteriora Libri Tertii Responsionem Exhibet: Posteriores Duo Francisco Suaresio Oppositi Sunt, Duosque Libros Eius de Scientia Dei Inscriptos Refellendos Suscipiunt. I. Alterum de Scientia Futurorum Contingentium Absoluta. II. Alterum de Scientia Futurorum Contingentium Conditionata.* Arnhem: Jacobum à Biesium, 1639.

Van Mastricht, Petrus. *Theoretico-Practica Theologia, Qua, Per Singula Capita Theologica, Pars Exegetica, Dogmatica, Elenchtica & Practica, Perpetuâ Successione Coniugantur.* Utrecht: Thomae Appels, 1699.

———. *Prolegomena.* Vol 1 of *Theoretical-Practical Theology.* Edited by Joel R. Beeke. Translated by Todd M. Rester. Grand Rapids: Reformation Heritage, 2018.

Vos, Antonie. "John Wesley on Salvation, Necessity, and Freedom." In *Evangelical Theology in Transition,* edited by Cornelis van der Kooi et al., 203–22. Amsterdam: VU University Press, 2012.

———. *The Philosophy of John Duns Scotus.* Edinburgh: Edinburgh University Press, 2006.

———. *The Theology of John Duns Scotus.* Studies in Reformed Theology 34. Leiden: Brill, 2018.

Bibliography

Vos, Geerhardus. "The Range of the Logos Title in the Prologue to the Fourth Gospel." In *Redemptive History and Biblical Interpretation: The Shorter Writings of Geerhardus Vos*, edited by Richard B. Gaffin Jr., 59–90. Phillipsburg, NJ: P. & R., 1980.

Watts, Isaac. *Logick: Or, the Right Use of Reason in the Inquiry after Truth. With a Variety of Rules to Guard against Error, in the Affairs of Religion and Human Life, as Well as in the Sciences*. 12th ed. London: Buckland & Longman, 1763.

Wesley, John. *A Compendium of Logic*. 2nd ed. London: 1756.

Willard, Samuel. *Compleat Body of Divinity in Two Hundred and Fifty Expository Lectures on the Assembly's Shorter Catechism*. Boston: Green & Kneeland, 1726.

Williams, Ebenezer. *A System of Ethicks and Pneumaticks. Of Morall Phylosophy in Generall & in Speciall*. Manuscript. From Harvard University Archives. 1707–8. https://nrs.harvard.edu/urn-3:HUL.ARCH:10919374?n=2.

Wippel, John F., and Allan B. Wolter, eds. *Medieval Philosophy: From St. Augustine to Nicholas of Cusa*. Readings in the History of Philosophy. New York: The Free Press, 1969.

Name Index

Abraham, 72, 74
Adam, 27, 38, 82
King Ahasuerus (Xerxes), 44
Alexander, H. G., 110n68,
    115nn157–162
Ames, William, xi, xivn1, 1–4, 10,
    75, 89, 91, 92, 101, 105n3,
    105n5, 105n7, 106n15,
    106n21, 109n56, 114n133,
    116n170, 116nn173–174,
    118n189
Andrew, Samuel, 69–70
Anselm, xii, xiii, xivn4
Aristotle, xi, xivn1, 91, 92, 109n62,
    116n170, 116n172,
    116n176
Arnauld, Antoine, 98, 108n51,
    109n55, 117n184
Asselt, Willem Jan van, 108n48,
    117n184, 118n187,
    118n191
Saint Augustine, 47, 49

Barnabas, 25–26
Barth, Karl, 116n168
Baudry, Léon, 109n59
Beck, Andreas J., 108n48,
    111nn90–91, 113n126,
    118n191
Beeke, Joel R., 107n24
Bellamy, Joseph, 118n188

Bellarmine, Robert, 110n63
Benson, Larry D., 110n72, 110n74,
    110n76
Boaz, 78
Boethius, 49, 50, 51, 110n76
Boso, xii
Bradwardine, Thomas, 47, 49,
    53–54, 55, 110nn74–75,
    111nn82–86
Bramhall, John, 31–36, 39, 65,
    108nn49–50, 109n54,
    109n55
Brattle, William, 117n185
Bulkeley, John 105n12
Burden, Mark, 106n17
Burgersdijk, Franco, 35, 89,
    109n56, 116n170, 116n171,
    116nn175–176
Burr, Aaron, 118n188
Burton, Simon, 113n126

Calvin, John, 113n126
Caroline, Princess of Wales, 83
Chappell, Vere, 108nn49–50, 109n54
Charnock, Stephen, 23–30, 37–38,
    39, 107nn39–40, 108nn43–
    47, 109nn59–60
Chaucer, Geoffrey, 47, 49–52,
    110n69, 110nn72–74,
    110n76, 111nn77–81
Christ. *See* Jesus Christ

Name Index

Clarke, Samuel, 7–8, 83, 105n12
Copernicus, 92
Criseyde, 51, 52

Damian, Peter, 67–68, 112n116, 113nn117–121
De Rivo, Peter, 109n59
Dekker, Eef, 118n190
Descartes, René, xi
Desiderius, Abbot, 67
Dryden, John, 47–48, 49, 110nn69–71
Duns Scotus, John, xiii, xivn5, 8, 35, 55, 66, 105–106n13, 108n53, 109n57, 112n115, 114n139
Dunster, Henry, 89–94

Edwards, Jonathan, xi, xii, 17–18, 73–80, 101, 103–104, 106n21, 107n30, 108n52, 113nn127–130, 114nn131–132, 114nn134–138, 114n140, 114nn142–151, 116n171, 118n188, 118nn192–195, 119n196
Edwards, Timothy, 99, 100
Queen Esther, 43–44
Eusden, 106n15
Euthyphro, 71
Eve, 27, 38
Ezekiel, 54

Fisk, Philip John, 105n12, 106n14, 106n21, 106n22, 107n36, 108nn49–50, 108n52, 109n54, 110n69, 111n92, 112n109, 114n139, 114n146, 115nn165–166, 116n170, 117nn177–182, 117n184, 118n188, 119n196

Gomarus, Franciscus, 9

Goodwin, Thomas, 15–16, 17, 19–20, 107nn24–29, 107nn31–35, 116n167

Hammond, Paul, 110nn69–71
Heereboord, Adriaan, xi, 13–14, 33, 59, 106n18, 106nn22–23, 111nn92–94, 112n95
Hermes, 25
Hezekiah, 26
Hobart, Nehemiah, 85
Hobbes, Thomas, xi, 31
Holifield, E. Brooks, 112n96
Hopkins, David, 110nn69–71

Isaac, 74

Saint James, 55
Jeremiah, 3, 64
Saint Jerome, 67
Jesus Christ, 2, 3, 5, 6, 15, 17, 18, 19, 20, 27, 28, 30, 38, 45, 64, 67, 74, 80, 100, 109n59
Job, 46, 72
Saint John, 5
John the Baptist, 64
Jones, Mark, 107n24
Judas, 77
Junius, Franciscus, 1, 3, 105n1, 105n8

Kennedy, Rick, 106n17
Kneale, Martha, 116n170, 117n183
Kneale, William, 116n170, 117n183
Knuuttila, Simo, 113n116, 118n192
Kuyper, Abraham, 6, 105n11

Lee, Sang Hyun 107n24
Leibniz, Gottfried Wilhelm, xi, 46, 81–84, 110n68, 115nn152–156
Leverett, John, 85–86, 117n185
Locke, John, xi

Name Index

Lombard, Peter, 114n139
Lovejoy, Arthur O., 118n192

Marenbon, John, 108n53, 109n53, 112n116
Mary (mother of Jesus), 78
Mather, Increase, 99–100
McClymond, Michael J., 107n24
Molina, Luis de, 85, 115n164
Mordecai, 44
Morison, Samuel Eliot, xivn1, 116n169, 117nn185–186
Morrison, Theodore, 110n73
Morton, Charles, xi, 11–12, 59–60, 85, 95–98, 99, 106n17, 106n18, 115n165
Moses, xiii, 58
Muller, Richard A., 111n87, 111n93, 114n139, 115n163, 115n166, 118n187

Newell, Daniel, 70, 113n123
Newton, 83
Nicole, Pierre, 98, 108n51, 109n55, 117n184
Novikoff, Alex J., xii, xivn2–3

Olivi, Peter John, 108n53, 109n53

Pascal, Blaise, xi
Saint Paul, 25–26, 29, 39–40, 41–42, 67
Pauw, Amy Plantinga 107n24
Saint Peter, 38, 109n59
Pharaoh, 13, 22
Plato, xi, xii, 113nn124–126
Pollmann, Karla, 116n167

Ramus, Peter, 89, 91, 92
Ruth, 78
Rutherford, Samuel, 39–44, 45, 109n61, 110nn63–66

Salmon (father of Boaz), 78

Saltonstall, G., 113n122
Saville, Henry, 55, 110n74
Schaff, Philip, 108nn41–42
Schoedinger, Andrew B., 109n59
Schweitzer, Don, 107n24
Socrates, 71
Solomon, 3
Spinoza, Baruch, 45
Stapfer, Johann Friedrich, 45–46, 106n21, 110nn66–67

Thachery, Peter, 109n58
Trelcatius, Lucas, Jr., 1–2, 3, 105n2, 105n4, 105n6, 106n16
Troilus, 51, 52
Turretin, Francis, 9, 115n167, 116n167, 118n187
Twisse, William, 55–56, 111nn88–89

van Mastricht, Peter, xi, 9–10, 21–22, 39, 81, 87–88, 107nn36–38, 115n167, 116n168
Veldhuis, Henri, 118n190
Voetius, Gisbertus, xi, 57–58, 59, 71–72, 102
Vos, Antonie 109n53, 114n139, 117n184
Vos, Geerhardus, 5–6, 105nn9–10

Watts, Isaac, 117n184, 119n196
Wesley, John, 117n184
Willard, Samuel, xi, 61–66, 106n21, 112nn96–108, 112nn110–114
Williams, Ebenezer, 106n18, 106nn19–20, 111n92, 111n94, 112n95, 115n165, 117nn177–182
Williams, Elisha, 101
Wippel, John F., 112n116, 113nn117–121
Wiswall, Samuel, 109n58

Name Index

Wolter, Allan B., 112n116, 113nn117–121

Zeus, 25

Scripture Index

OLD TESTAMENT

Genesis
1:1–3	46
1:3, 24, 26–27	6
1:24	6
1:26–27	6
1:31	84
2:1–3	84
3:8–13	38
6	24
6:5–8	24
6:6	23
6:19–20	92
16:13	12
18:16–33	72
45:5–8	62
50:20	82

Exodus
3:14	58, 68
9:12	14
10:1	22
14:17	14
21:12–13	104
25:9	3
33:17–23	60

Deuteronomy
2:30	76
5:6–22	56
6:4–15	32
29:29	2, 74

Joshua
24:15–28	96

1 Samuel
2:25	14
14:41	70
23:1–14	50

2 Kings
20:1–11	26

1 Chronicles
28:11, 12	3

2 Chronicles
7:14	28

Esther
3:13—5:3	44
4:15	44

Scripture Index

Job

9:32–33	46
12:10	36
13:3, 15	46
16:18–22	46
23:10–17	44
23:13	64
23:13–14	70
23:14	62
42:1–6	48

Psalms

11:5	8
16:5–11	104
16:11	56
19:1–14	92
19:7–11	72
24:1, 2	84
33:1–22	104
37:4	52
39:7–13	82
40:6–8	30
40:7–8	80
87:6	52
87:7	36
89:14	92
90:1–2	10
90:1–17	56
104:19–20, 29	22
105:16–25	76
115:3	8
116:12	80
119:89	62
131:1–3	48
135:6	62
139:1–18	48
147:5	2, 10

Proverbs

1:1–7	92
3:1–8	52
8:11–31	94
8:30	20

9:9–10	94
16:4	82
16:9	40
16:33	70
21:1	44
21:3	92
27:1	40
31:1–31	52

Song of Solomon

1:16	20

Isaiah

6:1–13	82
38:1–5	26
40:13, 14	58
42:1–4	80
43:1–28	54
43:25	66
44:7	82
48:1–22	54
50:5–9	80
53:10–12	78
55:6–9	48

Jeremiah

1:5	52
18:7–12	24
27:4–6	74
29:11	3
31:1–3	32
31:18–22	32
31:29	38
31:34	66
51:20–23	76

Lamentations

3:21–33	102
3:37–38	76, 104
3:37–66	8

Scripture Index

Ezekiel

18:1–32	38
18:20–12	28
36:22	54
36:22–32	54
36:26	64

Hosea

4:17	32
14:4	100

Jonah

2:4–10	28

Nahum

1:1–3	26

Habakkuk

2:2–3	12

Malachi

2:6	68
2:15 (KJV)	62
3:6	26

NEW TESTAMENT

Matthew

1:1–17	78
3:9	58
3:17	20
6:4	12
6:9–15	4, 50
6:10	104
10:29	62
11:4–6	34
11:20–24	86
11:25	64
11:26	16
11:27	10
20:16	64
26:26–28	90
26:26–29	90
26:31–75	50
26:36–56	78
26:41	96
26:53	58

Mark

1:40–41	34, 96
12:28–34	102

Luke

7:22	33
22:21–22	76
22:34	38
22:39–46	98
22:54–62	38

John

1:1	5
1:1–18	6
1:4, 9, 10	5
1:17	90
1:18	60
3:16	100
3:16–21	32
4:24	24
5:25–28	6
8:29	30, 96
8:58	68
10:17–18	30, 80
10:18	30
12:49	30
13:21–26	38
15:10	80
17:5–26	88
17:17	90
19:36	30
21:22	96

Scripture Index

Acts

2:23	74
3:12–21	74
5:31	66
14:11–15	25, 26
14:15 KJV	25
15:18	12
17:22–31	86
17:28	21, 22
27	39
27:1–44	40
27:43—28:6	42

Romans

1:18–25	4
2:3–5	74
2:14–15	4
3:4–6	72
4:5	34
5:8	18
5:12–17	38
6:14	66
7:7–25	98
8:2	66
8:28	46
9:5	24
9:13–26	70
11:29	66
11:33	2
11:34 KJV	29
12:1–2	102
16:25–27	102

1 Corinthians

1:26–3	104

2 Corinthians

4:16	100
5:7	11, 12, 42
11:2	67, 68

Ephesians

1:3–6	16
1:4	14
1:4, 9–10	18
1:4–7	88
1:5, 11	82
1:6–7	20
1:7	20
1:9–10	18
1:11	82
2:10	3
3:20	86
4:22, 24	64
4:24	64

Philippians

2:5–11	30
2:12, 13	64
2:13	34, 64

Colossians

1:15–17	60
2:3	8
2:9–10	4

1 Timothy

6:15–16	60

2 Timothy

2:19	14

Hebrews

1:3	4
4:15	80
6:17–20	80
7:22	28
9:15	28
11:1	42
11:3	46
12:2	64

James

1:13	56
1:17	24, 68
1:18	64
4:13–15	40
4:15	40
4:15 ESV	55
5:11	46
5:16–18	44

1 Peter

1:1–5	88
5:7	46

2 Peter

3:10–13	84

1 John

4:7–12	36

Revelation

4:11	14, 68
17:17	74

EARLY CHRISTIAN WRITINGS

Jerome	67
Augustine	47, 49

GRECO-ROMAN LITERATURE

Nicomachean Ethics

xivn1, 109n62

Posterior Analytics	116n172, 116n176
Plato, "Euthyphro"	113n124, 113n125

www.ingramcontent.com/pod-product-compliance
Lightning Source LLC
Chambersburg PA
CBHW070914160426
43193CB00011B/1452